HIDDEN HERITAGE

This catalogue is dedicated to the anonymous donor who sponsored the Georgia Decorative Arts Survey.

The exhibition *Hidden Heritage: Recent Discoveries in Georgia Decorative Art, 1733-1915* was on view at the High Museum of Art, Atlanta, Georgia, August 28-November 4, 1990. The exhibition was made possible in part by funds from The Citizens and Southern National Bank, with additional support from the Members Guild of the High Museum, Sotheby's, the Georgia Humanities Council, *Country Home Magazine*, and a gift in memory of Mrs. Carlyle Fraser. The catalogue was primarily supported by funds from The National Society of The Colonial Dames of America in the State of Georgia, with additional funding by anonymous gifts.

Edited by Katharine Gross Farnham,
    Margaret Miller, and Kelly Morris
Designed by Jim Zambounis
Type set by Katherine Gunn
Printed in Great Britain by
    Balding + Mansell International Ltd.
Copyright 1990 High Museum of Art
All rights reserved
Published 1990 by High Museum of Art
    Atlanta, Georgia
Library of Congress No. 90-81561
ISBN 0-939802-62-7

Cover: Detail of cat. no. 82.

HIDDEN HERITAGE

RECENT DISCOVERIES IN GEORGIA
DECORATIVE ART, 1733-1915

PAMELA WAGNER
GUEST CURATOR

MARY CAROLYN PINDAR
PHOTOGRAPHER

HIGH MUSEUM OF ART
ATLANTA
1990

LENDERS TO THE EXHIBITION

Anonymous lenders
Byron Attridge
Smith C. Banks
Mary Sue Jones Barron
Anne Brooks Bazemore
Mr. and Mrs. Fred D. Bentley, Sr.
H. Paul Blatner Antiques, Savannah
Mary Latimer Blue
Dr. and Mrs Charles G. Boland, Jr.
Edward G. and Mary Martin Davis Bowen
Ruth Barrow Bracewell
Dr. Josephine H. Brandon
Mr. and Mrs. Roger Bregenzer
Mrs. John Lawrence Brown
Pamela H. Bulman
Mrs. J. W. Butler
Leigh W. Brooks
Mrs. James J. Carswell
Mr. and Mrs. James D. Carter
Sara Mathis Chambers
Coastal Georgia Historical Society, St. Simons Island
Mr. and Mrs. Bayard McIntosh Cole
Mrs. Henry Latimer Collier, III
Mary Jane Hill Crayton
Charles R. Crisp
Mrs. Roper Bell David, Sr.
Martha Neal Dennis
Kellie Bush Dobbins
Mrs. John B. Echols, Sr.
Callie Huger Efird
Mr. and Mrs. William A. Fickling, Jr.
Jo Bailey Gladney
Mr. and Mrs. William W. Griffin
Mrs. Thomas T. Hawkins
Sylvia G. Head
Hattie Mina Reid Hicky
High Museum of Art
Ava Malaier Hill
Mrs. Morrill T. Hutchinson
Mr. and Mrs. Charles K. Johnston
Mr. and Mrs. A. Alling Jones
The Juliette Gordon Low Girl Scout National Center, Savannah
Martha LeBey Lassiter
Heath Laughlin, Jr.
Joe F. and Margaret S. Lawson, Jr.
James E. Lee, D.V.M.
Rabun A. (Alex) Lee, Jr.
Eugenia Selden Lehmann
Martha B. Long
The Martha Berry Museum of Berry College, Rome
Ben R. Maxwell
Ruth Mayo
Carolyn S. McMillan
Mrs. Alfred C. Nichols, Jr.

Isabelle C. Pitts
Mrs. Nell Tucker Popper
Mr. and Mrs. Joe Prather
Mr. and Mrs. Charles Nelson Pursley
Mrs. Mary Webb Rabey
William Edward Rudolph
Dr. and Mrs. Philip T. Schley
Dorothy Durrence Simmons
Mary Rucker Stewart
Mrs. Hugh Smiley Stanley
Fannie Laura Stowe
Robert B. and Winnie Tallant
Tallulah Falls School, Tallulah Falls
Louise Wise Teaford
The Telfair Academy of Arts and Sciences, Savannah
Thomas County Historical Society, Inc., Thomasville
Troup County Historical Society–Archives, La Grange
Mrs. Clyde J. Underwood
Margaret Hatcher Wagner
Augusta H. Warren
Dr. and Mrs. J. Herbert West
Mr. and Mrs. Broadus Estes Willingham IV
Mr. and Mrs. Kendall Zeliff

TABLE OF CONTENTS

Preface   PAGE   6

Acknowledgments   7

Foreword   9

Map of Georgia's Regions, Rivers, & Railroads   10

Introduction   11

The Tidewater Region: nos. 1-18   15

The Coastal Plain Region: nos. 19-43   29

Color Illustrations   49

The Piedmont Region: nos. 44-94   65

The Highlands Region: nos. 95-109   107

Bibliography   124

Index of Georgia Artisans   127

PREFACE

For over two decades the High Museum has been a leader in the study, collecting, and exhibition of Georgia decorative art. In 1971, Curator of Decorative Art Katharine G. Farnham and Museum Board member Callie Huger Efird organized a loan exhibition of American silver featuring a section on nineteenth-century Georgia silversmiths. In 1976, under the direction of guest curator Henry D. Green, Kitty Farnham and Callie Efird coordinated *Furniture of the Georgia Piedmont before 1830*. Since then, the Museum has established a Georgia collection, including significant examples of furniture, textiles, pottery, and metalwares.

The need for a statewide survey of Georgia's decorative art has been recognized from the time Henry D. Green first identified the unique qualities of Georgia-made furniture. But not until 1986 was such a project possible. In that year, an anonymous benefactor provided funds to support a three-year Georgia Decorative Arts Survey. This gift was made to The National Society of The Colonial Dames of America in the State of Georgia, who sponsored and organized the project.

The Georgia Decorative Arts Survey was conducted by Pamela Wagner, who focused her attention on recording pieces not previously published or exhibited, many still owned by descendants of their makers or original owners. This exhibition and its catalogue are the culmination of Ms. Wagner's more than twenty thousand miles of statewide travel and her recording of more than four thousand Georgia artifacts. Her research and this exhibition have benefitted from the support, effort, and facilities of the Colonial Dames, the Georgia Department of Archives and History, and the High Museum of Art. The entire record of Ms. Wagner's research will be presented to the Georgia Department of Archives and History to be used for future research.

The organizations and individuals who have been involved in the project are listed in Callie Efird's acknowledgments and Pamela Wagner's foreword. It is my pleasure to express the appreciation of the High Museum to each of them, thanking especially Pamela Wagner, the Colonial Dames, Catherine Tift Porter, the Georgia Department of Archives and History, the lenders to the exhibition, and Donald C. Peirce, the Museum's Curator of Decorative Art. We are very grateful to The Citizens and Southern National Bank, Sotheby's, the Georgia Humanities Council, *Country Home Magazine*, a friend of Mrs. Carlyle Fraser, and the Members Guild of the High Museum for their generous sponsorship of the exhibition, and to the Colonial Dames and anonymous donors for the publication of this catalogue. I note in particular the interest shown by Howard J. Morrison and Kirby A. Thompson at Citizens and Southern National Bank and by Virginia Beach and Katherine Ross at Sotheby's.

Finally, I wish to recognize and thank Kitty Farnham and Callie Efird once again for bringing to our museum audience the rich heritage of Georgia, and for their initial vision of a renaissance of the decorative arts at the High Museum.

Gudmund Vigtel
Director, High Museum of Art

ACKNOWLEDGMENTS

It is not often that a project receives the support and help of so many individuals across Georgia. The success of the Georgia Decorative Arts Survey is largely due to the people listed below, many of whom are members of The National Society of The Colonial Dames of America (NSCDA) in the State of Georgia. This group of women, through their seventeen Town Committees statewide, sponsored the survey, organizing and facilitating Pamela Wagner's visits, welcoming her into their homes, and introducing her to those in their own communities who could further the study. Each member's participation contributed also to the Dames' sponsorship of the exhibition catalogue.

To all the Dames and to the many others who have helped, we give sincere thanks. Specifically, I wish to recognize the following individuals and groups.

Our anonymous donor, a Dame known for her great generosity, whose interest in the history of Georgia and its decorative art have generated a rich resource for future study.

The National Society of The Colonial Dames of America in the State of Georgia Survey Committee: Mrs. William W. Farinholt, survey initiator and Co-chairman; Mrs. James T. Porter, Past Chairman of the Atlanta Town Committee, state board coordinator, and Survey Co-chairman; Mrs. Bernard T. Wolff, Vice-chairman and Past Chairman, Atlanta Town Committee; Mrs. Howard J. Morrison, Chairman, Atlanta Town Committee; Mrs. Shelby Myrick, Past President, NSCDA, Georgia; Mrs. Archie Morris, President, NSCDA, Georgia.

Atlanta Town Committee, Survey Committee: Mrs. James W. Bland, Jr., Mrs. Barry L. Frazier, Mrs. Peter G. Gantsoudes, Mrs. George B. Hightower, Mrs. Felton Jenkins, Jr., Mrs. V. Thomas Murray, and the late Mrs. William Rudolph.

High Museum of Art: Dorothy Anderson, Anna Bloomfield, Anne Brown, Colleen Callahan, Mickey Clark, Hilda Cyphers, Sue Deer, Margaret Denny, Ellen Dugan, Evan Forfar, Frances Francis, Sally Fulton, Leah Greenberg, Betsy Hamilton, Paula Hancock, Gail Harris, Marjorie Harvey, Elizabeth Hornor, Mike Jensen, Robert Leitch, Michael Manley, Maureen Marks, Margaret Miller, Kelly Morris, Alice Nightingale, Joy Patty, Tami Piggott, Mary Carolyn Pindar, Nancy Roberts, Laura Roe, Betty Sanders, Liesl Scheer, Suzanne Stedman, Teri Stewart, Naomi Vine, Jim Waters, Amanda Woods, Steve Woods, Midge Yearley, Jim Zambounis, and the decorative art volunteers.

Georgia Department of Archives and History: Dr. Edward Weldon, Director, and his staff.

Consultants: Mrs. and Mrs. William A. Parker, Jr.; Mr. and Mrs. Henry D. Green; Mr. and Mrs. William W. Griffin; Dr. Phinizy B. Spalding; Ms. Deanne Levison; Mr. Wendell Garrett; Mr. Charles Hummel, The Henry Francis du Pont Winterthur Museum; Mr. Bradford Rauschenberg, Museum of Early Southern Decorative Arts; and Ms. Jane Webb Smith.

Statewide Supporters: Mrs. Donald A. Cleesattle in Albany; Dr. and Mrs. John H. Robinson III, Mrs. Bonner M. Durham, Mr. and Mrs. George R. McMath, and Mrs. Henry L. Collier, III, in Americus; Mrs. C. Gordon Armstrong, Mrs. Hugh Gordon, Mrs. Dan H. DuPree, Mrs. George G. Miller, and Mrs. Samuel W. Wood in Athens; Mrs. Katharine

Phinizy Mackie, Mr. and Mrs. Clayton P. Boardman, Jr., and Mr. and Mrs. Bryan M. Haltermann in Augusta; Dr. and Mrs. T. Benjamin Youmans, Jr., in Calhoun; Mrs. Jefferson L. Davis in Cartersville; Mrs. Tony Hamilton and Mr. John Kollock in Clarkesville; Mrs. Jack F. King, Mrs. Barbara Swift Pound, and Mr. Clason Kyle in Columbus; Ms. Julia C. Lebsch in Gainesville; Mr. and Mrs. John H. Cheatham, Jr., in Griffin; Mrs. William L. Wood, Jr., Mrs. E. Wasden Bailey, Mrs. John L. Brown, and Mrs. Bert D. Schwartz in Macon; Mr. and Mrs. W. Graham Ponder and Mrs. Lowry W. Hunt in Madison; Mrs. Henry S. Brown, Jr., Mrs. Norman M. Shipley, and Mrs. Elyea D. Carswell, Jr., in Marietta; Mr. and Mrs. J. L. Sibley Jennings, Mr. and Mrs. John E. Garner, Jr., Mrs. Herbert N. Chandler, Mrs. Joseph R. Uhler, and Miss Mary Jo Thompson in Milledgeville; Mrs. Hoyt H. Whelchel, Jr., Mrs. Jack C. Smith, Mrs. Ladson Vereen, and Mr. and Mrs. Keith Murphy in Moultrie; Mrs. Bernard N. Neal, Dr. and Mrs. Harlan M. Starr, Jr., Mrs. Stephen D. Smith, and Mrs. James D. Maddox in Rome; Mr. and Mrs. William S. Burdell, Jr., Mrs. Talmadge M. Baumgardner, Mr. and Mrs. U. Shasta McCranie, and Mrs. William Q. Walker, Jr., in St. Simons; Mr. and Mrs. Benjamin J. Tarbutton, Jr., in Sandersville; Mrs. Henry F. Garlington, Mr. and Mrs. Peter M. Coy, Mrs. Beverly E. Leigh, Mrs. Edgar P. Williams, Mrs. Caroline Jones Wright, Mr. and Mrs. Martin L. Karp, and Mrs. M. Heyward Mingledorff in Savannah; Mr. and Mrs. William P. Selman in Summersville; Mrs. John A. Bracey, Jr., Mrs. John Bracey, Sr., Mrs. Lonnie D. Ferguson, Miss Margaret Evans, and Mrs. Thomas T. Hawkins in Thomasville; Mrs. Adair Myddleton Nunnally, Dr. and Mrs. Henry B. Smith, and Mrs. Frederick L. Smotherman, Jr., in Valdosta; Mrs. James E. Reynolds in Washington; and Mrs. Alvin M. Ratliff and Mrs. John Augustus Shields, Jr., in Waycross.

I wish to recognize especially Gudmund Vigtel, Director of the High Museum, who, from the inception of this survey, had the vision to offer the Museum's support and encouragement. Donald C. Peirce, the Museum's Curator of Decorative Art, also deserves thanks for his wise counsel and his ability to analyze and craft prose.

Most importantly, I salute our survey director, Pamela Wagner, who had the courage and energy to tackle many unknowns. Her insatiable curiosity and abundant good humor have endeared her to people in every corner of our state. May this transplanted Georgian's few years with us stand her in good stead wherever and whenever.

Finally, two other individuals, each of whom made a three-year commitment to this project, deserve special accolades. For their patience and perseverance, and for countless hours of dedication to detail, my thanks go to Catherine Tift Porter, the gracious Dames coordinator and survey co-chairman, and to my longtime associate Katharine Gross Farnham, the Museum's liaison to the survey and coordinator of the exhibition and catalogue.

Callie Huger Efird
Board of Directors, High Museum of Art
Treasurer, Georgia Decorative Arts Survey, Atlanta Town
Committee, The National Society of The Colonial Dames in America
in the State of Georgia

FOREWORD

At the inception of the Georgia Decorative Arts Survey, the Colonial Dames could not have anticipated the scope of the project they were undertaking. Their survey would reveal four thousand documented artifacts made in Georgia before 1915, one hundred nine of which are presented in the exhibition *Hidden Heritage*.

My fieldwork can be viewed as Georgia's largest tour of homes—I visited more than nine hundred. First, I wish to thank everyone who invited me to stay with them and become part of their lives. Their hospitality and dedication to my work contributed significantly to its success. To all the people I interviewed, my thanks for taking time to show me family heirlooms and to share family stories.

Being on the road has advantages over working nine-to-five in an office. My travels allowed me to participate in oyster roasts on the coastal islands and a Mystery Club weekend in Valdosta, and led me to discover northwest Georgia's viniculture. I will cherish these and other memories whenever thinking about Georgians, many of whom will remain good friends.

Researching the entries for the catalogue was often laborious. Special thanks go to my colleagues at the Georgia Department of Archives and History for their guidance to specialized sources. I am also indebted to probate judges and to Superior Court clerks and their assistants for retrieving legal records, and to museum and historical society professionals around the state for their interest and assistance. Sincere thanks also to the descendants of the artisans and original owners, who answered a myriad questions in person, over the phone, and by mail.

I benefitted greatly from the professional expertise and friendship of the staff of the High Museum. My sincere thanks to them and especially to catalogue photographer Mary Carolyn Pindar, whose talent and aesthetic sense are apparent in the illustrations.

I wish to also thank my four interns, Yvonne Lindsey, Elizabeth DuBose, Julia Waterfill, and Lillian Gantsoudes, who brought diligence, patience, and good humor to the task of preparing the documentary files for presentation to the Archives. The Archives administrative support staff generously shared their technical knowledge, enabling me to computerize the artifact records.

I dedicate this catalogue to the anonymous donor who generously funded the survey. Callie Efird, from the first day, provided guidance and encouragement. She became my surrogate mother, calling to make sure I got back to town safely. Kitty Farnham gave me professional advice on documentation and often served as an unknowing role model in dealing with difficult people in difficult situations. I appreciated her assistance during the research, writing, and editing of this catalogue, work often carried out on very little sleep. Where would I have been without Tee Porter's assistance as the Dames' state coordinator, scheduling my visits with scores of Dames around Georgia? All her phone calls kept me going to the right place at the right time—if it's Tuesday, it must be Enigma. The generosity, foresight, perseverance, and inspiration of these four ladies made the survey and exhibition a reality.

Pamela Wagner
Director, Georgia Decorative Arts Survey

MAP OF GEORGIA'S REGIONS, RIVERS, & RAILROADS

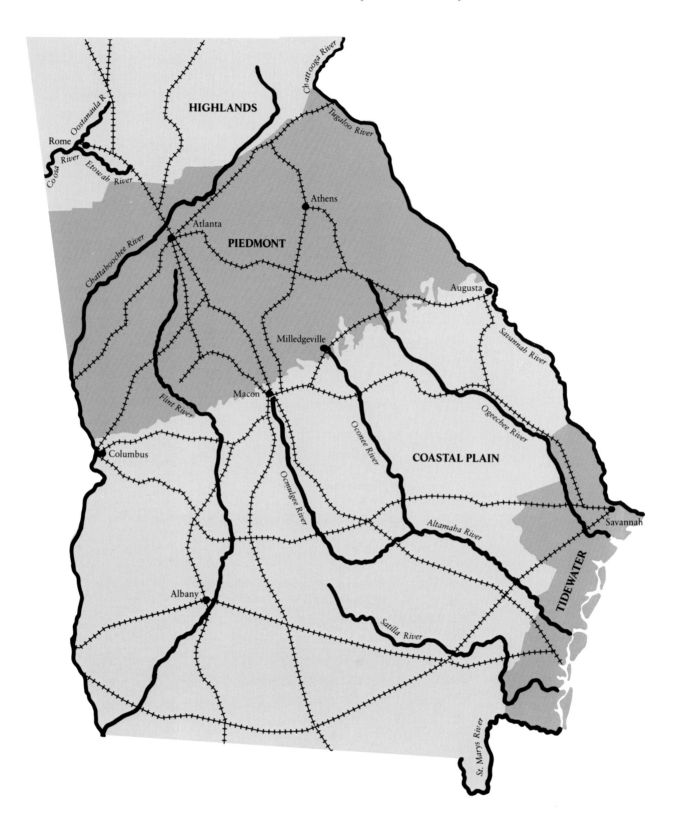

INTRODUCTION

As Georgia's historic artifacts have passed from generation to generation, and from seller to buyer, many have lost their histories and been
removed from their original contexts. To protect what survives of this
tangible evidence of Georgia's cultural history, The National Society of
The Colonial Dames of America in the State of Georgia initiated the
Georgia Decorative Arts Survey in 1986.

The survey was designed to locate, document, and photograph previously unrecorded objects made in Georgia from the time of English
settlement in 1733 to World War I, recording data about the makers and
original owners of these pieces. The goal of the survey was to create a
resource file—rich with family histories and object photographs—to
provide raw material for new research, exhibitions, and publications
about Georgia's decorative art. The Georgia Department of Archives
and History was selected as the repository for these records, so that they
might be permanently available to researchers. To encourage the owners
of artifacts to participate, their anonymity was assured.

As a part of their commitment to historic preservation in Georgia, the
Colonial Dames established the survey and helped with its implementa-
tion. An anonymous gift from an individual Dame underwrote three
years of fieldwork. The Atlanta Town Committee organized Dames
from each of the other sixteen town committees in Georgia to publicize
the survey, distribute questionnaires, and provide assistance and hospitality to the survey director.

In the fall of 1986, museum and historical society representatives,
archivists, and professional historians from the fields of decorative art,
architectural, social, and economic history, and archaeology met at the
Georgia Department of Archives and History in Atlanta. Their assistance and advice were sought in defining the boundaries of the survey. It
was decided to focus on interior furnishings—furniture, textiles, metalwares, ceramics, and glass.

The search for Georgia-made artifacts began when questionnaires
were distributed statewide by the Dames and by the participants in the
Archives meeting. An article in the *Atlanta Journal and Constitution*
invited Georgians to send in descriptions of their artifacts. Before long,
over a thousand responses had been received. At this point, the survey
focused upon those pieces for which makers or early Georgia owners
could be identified. Objects believed to have been made in Georgia, but
which lacked histories or documentation, were rarely recorded. To save
time and to concentrate on gathering new information, objects previously published or accessible in museum and historical society
collections were not included.

During two years of fieldwork, the Georgia Decorative Arts Survey
recorded more than 4,300 objects at approximately 870 sites in seventy-
three Georgia counties. The documentation of each object included a
written description, measurements, a brief condition report, and the history of the artisan and the object's early owners. The information was
entered on a portable computer, using a program designed with the
assistance of the technical support staff at the Georgia Department of
Archives and History. The program was based on registration forms
used in the decorative arts photographic collection at the Henry Francis
du Pont Winterthur Museum in Delaware and in the field research sur-

veys of the Museum of Early Southern Decorative Arts in Winston-Salem, North Carolina. Drawer construction was recorded for most case pieces using a modification of a form designed by the Museum of Early Southern Decorative Arts. Black and white photographs of each piece were taken; color slides were made of textiles, ceramics, and painted and grained furniture.

As the survey period ended, an exhibition was planned to publicize this extensive new record of Georgia artifacts and to present some of the significant discoveries. It is hoped that the exhibition and catalogue will increase the general understanding of Georgia's decorative art and will stimulate further research.

Most of the pieces in the exhibition are from private collections and have descended in the families of the makers or original owners. Family histories and oral traditions concerning the artifacts were recorded whenever available. This information generally consisted of the name and life dates of the artisan or ancestor and was usually drawn from family-owned Bibles, genealogy records, or patriotic service organization records. For this catalogue, extensive additional research was done using such primary sources as military records, federal population and census records, state manufacturing censuses, wills, inventories and appraisements of estates, and land records. Secondary sources—published and unpublished family histories, city and county histories, and biographies—were also consulted.

The exhibition is organized by geographic regions of the state—the Tidewater, the Coastal Plain, the Piedmont, and the Highlands—which are distinct in their settlement patterns and in the raw materials available to local craftsmen. By examining these artifacts where they were made and where most remain today, the works will be better understood in relation to other artifacts of each region and of neighboring regions and states.

Most of the objects in the exhibition date from the nineteenth century. Of the more than 4,300 objects recorded, only a few dated from the first century after the English settlement of Georgia. The lack of early artifacts can be attributed to the ravages of wars, fires, storms, and floods in the eighteenth and nineteenth centuries. Many early pieces undoubtedly were transported out of the state. During the Revolutionary War, Loyalists moved to England, Canada, Florida, and the West Indies. Later, during the nineteenth century, settlers migrated to Alabama, Mississippi, Texas, Oklahoma, and Arkansas. In the twentieth century, antique dealers, both southern and northern, purchased family heirlooms from Georgians and sold them out-of-state, often unaware of their distinctive regional character. It is hoped that the Georgia origin of some of these pieces may someday be determined.

Most of the 2,300 documented pieces of furniture were simple and conservative in style. A few high-style objects from the nineteenth century suggest awareness of furniture fashions being produced in northern cities. The furniture was made of local woods, including walnut, tulip poplar, white and yellow pines, cherry, hickory, chestnut, cypress, birch, and cedar; mahogany was the most commonly used non-native wood. Cabinetmakers added a variety of surface finishes, either for aesthetic refinement or to unify a piece fashioned from different woods. Paint colors included ocher, Spanish brown (resembling terra cotta), reddish orange, medium and dark greens, oyster white, black, pale blue, and deep marine blue. Graining, another popular surface treatment, was applied with a paintbrush, comb, or sponge, to simulate mahogany, rosewood, and oak.

Curly pine, with its unusual, highly figured grain, was one of the survey's most interesting finds (see cover and nos. 36, 82, and 84). Scientists have offered several explanations for this characteristic grain. It may be due to a genetic irregularity within the dividing cells of the cambial layer under the bark, causing an abnormal growth pattern; it may be caused by injury to a young tree, the result of a wound or fungus; or it could result from stress to a young seedling bending toward a light source obstructed by large trees.[1] Furniture made of curly pine was recorded in the Tidewater and Coastal Plain regions, and near Augusta. In the Tifton area, curly pine was also found in interior woodwork such as china closets, bookcases, window seats, newel posts, and wood paneling. All the recorded curly pine pieces date from the late nineteenth and early twentieth centuries, and tend to be more sophisticated in design than other pieces of similar provenance, suggesting that the figured wood was considered stylish.

The survey recorded nearly seven hundred textile items—samplers, embroidery, and bedcovers. Because most of these textiles were made for use in the family and have descended to succeeding generations, the makers can be identified. Most pieces are in good condition, having been stored in trunks or blanket chests, protected from the dangers of regular use, sunlight, and insects. The largest group of recorded textiles were bedcovers, including appliquéd chintz quilts dating from the 1820s to the 1850s, mid-to-late-century pieced quilts using solid cottons and printed calicos, and later crazy quilts. Approximately one hundred late-nineteenth-century crocheted, knitted, or drawnwork bedcovers were found. Also recorded were loom-woven coverlets, worked in wool and cotton, in a diversity of patterns. Georgia samplers are very scarce; approximately one dozen dating from the first half of the nineteenth century were recorded. In addition, hundreds of handworked table linens were seen, but not included in this survey.

Approximately seven hundred objects of silver, pewter, gold, iron, brass, and tin were documented. Many of the silver entries contain a group of related objects under one number—for example, six tablespoons from a set, each having the same maker's mark or owner's monogram. Although nearly two hundred silversmiths and watchmakers are known to have been working in Georgia between 1733 and 1850, almost no hollow ware was found. Noteworthy metal objects in the exhibition include an eighteenth-century cloak stud from Ebenezer (no. 1), the earliest object recorded during the survey, a rare piece of Georgia-made pewter (no. 45), and a five-dollar gold coin minted in Dahlonega (no. 102).

Close to seven hundred ceramic items were recorded. Many more pieces of Georgia-made pottery were examined but not recorded because they have already been well documented.[2] Included in the exhibition are a stoneware bowl (no. 38) and a stoneware vase with an unusual "Rockingham" mottled glaze (no. 76). The survey also recorded European porcelain tablewares painted by Georgians in the late nineteenth and early twentieth centuries. The craft of china painting was an offshoot of the international Arts and Crafts movement, which encouraged the revival of handwork (see nos. 34, 91, 92, 93, and 94).

As a result of my fieldwork, I am convinced that these recent discoveries represent only a fraction of what must have been made in the state. Tantalizing requests to document other pieces are still being received. It is my hope that the Georgia Decorative Arts Survey files at the Georgia

Department of Archives and History will draw many researchers and scholars to study these artifacts, to help reconstruct Georgia's artistic, cultural, social, and economic past. Among the decorative arts topics inviting further study in Georgia are the practice of painting and graining furniture and interior architecture; textile handwork; artifacts made by African-Americans, barely represented in this survey; iron foundries and their production of furniture and architectural ornament; and the art schools and studios where china painting was taught. As this exhibition and future studies expand our knowledge and appreciation of Georgia's crafts and craftsmen, perhaps we can hope for a Georgia museum of history, technology, and culture to provide a permanent home for the state's historic artifacts before they are irretrievably lost.

Pamela Wagner
Director, Georgia Decorative Arts Survey

1. Information based upon phone conversations with Leon A. Hargraves, Jr., Dean of the School of Forest Resources, University of Georgia, Athens, Georgia; and Kemp McDonald, Researcher, and Donna Christensen, Botanist, at the Forest Products Laboratory, Madison, Wisconsin.
2. John Burrison, *Brothers in Clay: The Story of Georgia Folk Pottery* (Athens, Ga.: University of Georgia Press, 1983); and Suzanne Harper et al., *Georgia Clay: Pottery of the Folk Tradition* (Macon: Museum of Arts and Sciences, 1989).

NOTES ON CATALOGUE ENTRIES

Works selected for this exhibition have strong Georgia provenances, based on marks (signatures or inscriptions) or family histories linking the maker, original owner, or early owner to residency in the state.

Works are arranged in loose chronological order within regions. *Circa* placed before a range of dates (e.g., ca. 1736-1755) indicates a conviction that the work was made sometime during the period—not before, not after.

Primary woods—that is, visible materials—are listed first. Secondary woods (framing, interior, or otherwise not readily seen materials) are listed after a semicolon. Woods were identified by field examination, not laboratory analysis.

Silver marks are described either as incised (cut into the metal) or stamped (hammered in, leaving the letters raised).

Dimensions are given in inches, height before width before depth. In textiles, length is given before width. No depth is given for corner cabinets.

THE TIDEWATER REGION

The Tidewater is the low-lying coastal region which includes fifteen barrier islands and the adjacent mainland counties. Flowing through the region are five of the state's major rivers—the Savannah, Ogeechee, Altamaha, Satilla, and St. Marys—which form marshy deltas. The Savannah and the St. Marys form Georgia's natural boundaries with South Carolina and Florida.

English settlers, led by General James Oglethorpe, founded Savannah in 1733. A year later, the Salzburgers arrived, fleeing religious persecution in Austria and other Germanic states. They settled primarily in Ebenezer, twenty miles upriver from Savannah. After the American Revolution, French-speaking emigrants from France, Acadia (Canada), and Santo Domingo came to the Tidewater port cities: first to Sunbury and Savannah, and later to St. Marys and Brunswick. In the nineteenth century, the Irish constituted the largest immigrant population, concentrating in Savannah. Throughout the period, Americans from northern and neighboring states also settled in the region's towns. African slaves were brought to the Tidewater shortly after white settlement, and by the end of the Revolutionary War outnumbered white residents within the region.

Transportation played a pivotal role in the development of the coastal economy. The Savannah River provided a navigable route between Augusta and Savannah. As steamships became commonplace, all five Tidewater rivers became busy waterways, moving crops, raw materials, and merchandise. By these routes, settlers moved inland from the coast. In 1843, the Central of Georgia Railroad line was completed, providing another important link between the state's largest coastal port, Savannah, and the inland agricultural areas. Later rail lines connected Savannah to Augusta and to Thomasville, and linked the port of Brunswick with Waycross. Particularly after the Civil War, these railroads prompted the establishment of lumber mills in the Coastal Plain region, and brought lumber to the ports of Brunswick, Darien, and Savannah.

The Tidewater ports, especially Savannah, had close mercantile connections with cities to the north, including Boston, Newport, New York, Philadelphia, Baltimore, and Charleston. Ships brought mail, news, supplies, raw materials, manufactured goods, and settlers. Regular contact with these other ports kept Savannah abreast of the latest fashions.

Fieldwork carried out in the earliest settled districts of Georgia—Ebenezer, Savannah, Brunswick, and St. Simons Island—has revealed little that can be firmly attributed to the region's eighteenth-century craftsmen. Furniture having a Tidewater provenance is scarce. Although the port of Savannah had almost forty cabinetmakers between 1789 and 1815, little of their work can be positively identified today.[1] However, this survey recorded five pieces by one mid-nineteenth-century cabinetmaker, John Wilkins (see no. 10).

A wide range of handmade bedcoverings were found in the Tidewater region. English or French roller-printed textiles were used in appliquéd chintz quilts dating from the 1820s and 1830s (see no. 5). Mid-century pieced and appliquéd quilts were made from solid and printed cottons, both domestic and imported. Late-nineteenth-century crazy quilts were fabricated in rich velvets, silks, and satins (no. 14). The crocheted and knitted openwork found in other regions was not found in the Tidewater. Of the twelve samplers recorded in the survey, six were from the Tidewater (see nos. 6, 7, 9).

Many of the silver objects documented during the survey bore marks of Savannah artisans, reflecting the number of silver craftsmen working in that community.[2] Although most of the silver pieces found were flatware, a few hollow ware items were also documented, including tea services, water pitchers, goblets, and a toast rack. Georgia's earliest known silver object originated in the Tidewater, a cloak stud (no. 1) made by Freidrich Wilhelm Müller of Ebenezer between 1736 and 1751. Other noteworthy pieces from Savannah are sugar tongs (no. 3) by John Ogier, the first marked piece found by him, and a spoon (no. 4) crafted by F. Eastman, a previously unknown maker. An iron gate cast at Kehoe and Company (no. 16) represents the later period of Savannah's iron industry.

The Tidewater region failed to yield new discoveries in Georgia-made pottery or glass. Foreign and coastal imports probably met most of the demands of local customers, so little was produced here. Local archaeological digs have uncovered glass bottles and jars from northern and European glassworks.

Only a few artifacts made by African-Americans were found in the Tidewater area. These included bedcoverings, furniture, and a gravemarker (no. 17).

1. Katharine Wood Gross, "The Sources of Furniture Sold in Savannah, 1789-1815" (Master's thesis, University of Delaware, 1967), pp. 17-47. See also Mrs. Charlton M. Theus, *Savannah Furniture, 1733-1825* (Savannah, 1967).
2. The most thorough listing of Georgia silversmiths can be found in George Barton Cutten, *The Silversmiths of Georgia* (Savannah: The Pigeonhole Press, 1958).

1

Cloak or Coat Stud

Ebenezer, Effingham County, ca. 1736-1751
Made by Freidrich Wilhelm Müller (ca. 1690-ca. 1751)
Silver
$\frac{1}{2}$ x $\frac{7}{8}$ x $\frac{7}{8}$ inches
Marks: "MULLER" stamped on bottom
Private collection

Eighteenth-century Georgia-made silver is extremely rare. This cloak or coat stud made by Freidrich Wilhelm Müller is the earliest known piece, and is one of the few colonial Georgia artifacts with a documented history of having been made by a resident of the Salzburger settlement of Ebenezer, up the river from Savannah.[1]

The Salzburgers, along with many Moravians and Palatines, came to America to escape religious persecution. Most of what is known of the Salzburger community and of Freidrich Müller comes from the daily journals kept by Johann Martin Boltzius and Israel Christian Gronau, ministers of Ebenezer, who kept the official records of the sectarian settlement's activities beginning in 1733. Müller, a Palatine, arrived in Georgia in February 1736 with Von Reck on the sixth Salzburger transport, *Merchant*.[2]

Müller trained as a clockmaker in Germany, but his talents were many. Journal entries repeatedly acknowledge his abilities: "This clockmaker is actually a papermaker who additionally learned to make wooden clocks and has also practiced other kinds of mechanics. . . . He can make almost anything that he sees; and he works not only in wood but also in bone, iron and other tractable things."[3] It was recorded that Müller requested "a mold for pouring pewter spoons and also strong wire for hackling flax." He made

spinning wheels, and, having obtained deer horns from Indian women, used his lathe to fashion buttons and knife handles. One of Müller's most important commissions was noted in the 1741 journals: "six striking clocks for General Oglethorpe in Frederica."[4]

From this remarkably industrious and talented craftsman, only one identifiable piece survives—this silver stud with its engraved quatrefoil design and clear maker's mark.

1. George Fenwick Jones, *The Salzburger Saga* (Athens, Ga.: University of Georgia Press, 1984), p. 14.
2. Samuel Urlsperger, George Fenwick Jones, and Marie Hahn, eds., *Detailed Reports of The Salzburger Emigrants Who Settled in America*, vol. 3, 1736, (Athens, Ga.: University of Georgia Press, 1972), p. 104. See also George Fenwick Jones, *The Germans of Colonial Georgia, 1733-1783* (Baltimore: Geneological Publishing Co., Inc., 1986), p. 176.
3. George Fenwick Jones and Renate Wilson, eds., *Detailed Reports of The Salzburger Emigrants*, vol. 5, 1738, pp. 111, 186-87.
4. George Fenwick Jones, ed., *Detailed Reports of The Salzburger Emigrants*, vol. 8, 1741, p. 41.

2

Dining Table End

One of a pair
Probably Savannah, Chatham County, ca. 1815
Made by unknown artisan
Mahogany, mahogany veneers, and inlays;
yellow pine
29 x 52 x 25½ inches
Descent in family of original owner
The Coastal Georgia Historical Society

Previous surveys have identified only a few pieces of
furniture made in the Savannah area in the eighteenth
and early nineteenth centuries. However, contemporary newspaper advertisements indicate that at least
forty cabinetmakers were there between 1789 and
1815.[1] This survey found only these table ends by
an unknown maker and several later pieces by John
Wilkins (see no. 10).

The estate inventory and appraisal of Anna Matilda
Page King, dated February 24, 1860, lists "1 dining
table." Anna Matilda Page King, the daughter of
Hannah Timmons and Major William Page, was
raised at Retreat Plantation, St. Simons Island, which

had been purchased by her parents in 1804. Shortly
after her marriage in 1824 to Thomas Butler King of a
neighboring plantation, both her parents died, leaving
her sole heir to their vast estate. These table ends are
not detailed in her parents' wills but possibly came
into her possession at the time of their deaths. The
table ends were acquired by the Coastal Georgia Historical Society from Butler King Couper, a descendant
of Anna Page King.

The pair of table ends along with a center drop-leaf
section formed the full table, making it possible to set
up the table in various configurations. The use of
imported mahogany and mahogany veneers over a
base of local yellow pine is not surprising, particularly on furniture made in coastal areas. The table
skirt has light string inlay; a wide band of darker
inlay marks the cuffs near the lower edge of the legs.

1. Katharine Wood Gross, "The Sources of Furniture Sold
   in Savannah, 1789-1815" (Master's Thesis, University of
   Delaware, 1967), pp. 17-47.

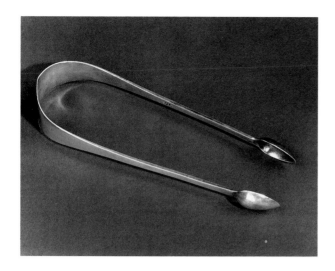

3

SUGAR TONGS

Savannah, Chatham County, ca. 1808-1814
Made by John Ogier (1761-1814)
Silver
5½ inches long
Marks: "J.O" in rectangle stamped on inside
of shafts; "ET" engraved on outside
Descent in family of original owner
Lent by H. Paul Blatner Antiques, Savannah

The silversmith John Ogier was working in Baltimore
in 1787, in New York City around 1791, in Norfolk,
Virginia, in 1803, and in Charleston, South Carolina,
before settling in 1808 in Savannah, where he
remained until his death in 1814.[1] These unadorned
tongs are the only known item which bears his
hallmark.

The initials engraved on the tongs are probably
those of Ebenezer Tubbs (1790-1820), in whose family the utensil descended. A native of Connecticut,
Tubbs had moved to Savannah by 1809, when he married Harriet Vallotton.

1. Ralph M. Kovel and Terry H. Kovel, *A Directory of
   American Silver, Pewter and Silver Plate* (New York:
   Crown Publishers, Inc., 1961), p. 201.

4

DESSERT SPOON

Savannah, Chatham County, ca. 1825-1850
Made by F. Eastman
Silver
7 inches long
Marks: "F. EASTMAN" in rectangle stamped
on back of spoon
Lent by H. Paul Blatner Antiques, Savannah

This is the first piece of silver found bearing the mark
of F. Eastman, a previously unknown Savannah
silversmith who possibly was related to Moses Eastman, a known smith working in Savannah between
1826 and 1850. This dessert spoon was unearthed in
Chippewa Square, opposite 17 West McDonough
Street, where Moses Eastman lived between 1844
and 1847. Census records show no Eastman with the
initial "F."

The design of the spoon, with its basket of flowers
on the handle, suggests a date in the second quarter of
the nineteenth century.

5

QUILT

Savannah, Chatham County, before 1821
Made by Ann Legardere Clay (1745-1821)
Cotton
98 x 94½ inches
Descent in family of maker
High Museum of Art, gift of Helen Stiles Rose
Color illustration on page 49

This Tree of Life quilt is one of the earliest known
Savannah-made quilts. As was common practice in
this period, trees, flowers, butterflies, and birds were
cut from colorful chintz fabrics, rearranged into the
Tree of Life design, and appliquéd to a solid ground,
usually white cotton. Imported from England or
France, the chintzes were block-printed, copper-
engraved, or roller-printed, and derived their designs
from *palampores*, fabrics that were brought to
Europe from India.

Ann Legardere Clay was born in Yorktown, North
Carolina. In 1763 she married Joseph Clay, who
became a distinguished member of the Savannah
Council of Safety, the Provincial Congress, and a
trustee of the State College. Clay owned a counting
house and had a very profitable mercantile business
in Savannah.[1]

According to family tradition, this is one of several
quilts which Ann made. A sampler stitched by her
granddaughter, Eliza Caroline Clay, is also in this
exhibition (see no. 6).

1. Harvey H. Jackson and Phinizy Spalding, eds., *Forty
   Years of Diversity: Essays on Colonial Georgia*
   (Athens, Ga.: University of Georgia Press, 1984),
   pp. 205, 209, 252.

6

SAMPLER

Bryan County, Georgia, or Medford,
Massachusetts, 1817
Made by Eliza Caroline Clay (1809-1895)
Linen and silk
16³⁄₄ x 16¹⁄₄ inches
Marks: "Eliza Caroline Clay's work. 1817./
August 6. aged 8 years." embroidered at bottom
Descent in family of maker
Private collection

Eliza Caroline Clay was the youngest child of Mary
Ann Savage and Joseph Clay of Tranquilla Plantation
near Richmond, Georgia. Her paternal grandmother
was Ann Legardere Clay (see no. 5). After her father's
death in 1811, Eliza's family lived primarily in
Medford, Massachusetts, but retained close ties to
their Georgia relatives. By 1825 Eliza had returned to
Georgia to live permanently on the family plantation,
Richmond-on-Ogeechee.

Georgia-made samplers are extremely rare. A
dozen were documented for the Georgia Decorative
Arts Survey, most of which have embroidered upper
and lower case alphabets followed by the numbers
zero to nine. All were signed and some dated by their
makers. Additional ornamentation includes land-
scapes, scattered flowers, and occasionally a verse,
as in this case.

7

SAMPLER

Savannah, Chatham County, 1824
Made by Mary Elizabeth Vallotton Wells (1810-1891)
Linen and silk
16¹⁄₄ x 15³⁄₄ inches
Marks: "Mary. Elizabeth. Vallotton. ended/this.
Sampler. July. 16. 1824" embroidered at bottom
Descent in family of maker
Lent by Anne Brooks Bazemore
Color illustration on page 49

The name and date on this sampler indicate that Mary
Elizabeth Vallotton completed the work when she was
fourteen years old. Her descendants who own this
sampler also own two quilts made by her great-grand-
mother, Johanna Christiana Miller (1765-1826); one
is an appliquéd Tree of Life pattern and the other has
appliquéd floral sprigs arranged in a block pattern.
Another branch of the family owns a verse sampler
worked by one of Mary Elizabeth's sisters, but the
name and date have faded and are illegible.

Very little is known about Mary Elizabeth. She
was the second of nine children born to Elizabeth
Lavender Miller and Paul Jonathan Vallotton, a cord-
wainer. In 1828 she married William H. Wells. They
had four children: Francis Oliver, Elizabeth, Eleanor
Anne, and James Edward Patterson.

8

TOAST RACK

Savannah, Chatham County, or New York City,
ca. 1819-1831
Made by Frederick Marquand (1799-1882)
Silver
5¼ x 6¾ x 4⅝ inches
Marks: "F.M.," profile of head, "G," lion passant
in boxes stamped on underside of base; "Eliza"
engraved in oval medallion under handle
The Telfair Academy of Arts and Sciences, Savannah,
purchase, 1980

Most early Georgia silversmiths are known today
only by a few marked spoons or forks. Frederick
Marquand is an exception. An abundance of flatware
and a variety of hollow ware forms (including tea
sets, a pitcher, and a porringer) survive bearing
his marks.

Although common in England, the toast rack was
a rare form in American silver. Only seven early nineteenth-century American-made examples exist, and
this is the only one bearing the mark of a silversmith
who worked in Savannah.

Marquand worked in Savannah from 1819 to 1826,
then moved to New York. He used this mark while
in Savannah and may have continued using it for the
first five years in New York. Hence, works made
between 1819 and 1831 cannot be precisely dated.[1] All
history of ownership of this piece is lost.

1. For a discussion of Marquand, see Jane Webb Smith,
   Georgia's Legacy: History Charted Through the Arts
   (Athens, Ga.: University of Georgia Press, 1985),
   pp. 209-11. William W. Griffin, Atlanta, has established
   that Marquand was at work in Savannah by 1819.

9

SAMPLER

St. Marys, Camden County, 1833
Made by Mary Frances Victorine DeBrot
Linen and silk
24¾ x 21¾ inches
Marks: "Mary Frances Victorine DeBrot/St. Mary's,
Georgia/1833" embroidered at the bottom
High Museum of Art, purchase with funds from
The Decorative Arts Endowment

Embroidered on this sampler are flowers above a
wavy band with a landscape below, all within a floral
motif border.

Very little is known about Mary Frances Victorine
DeBrot. In the 1830 Federal Census, her parents,
Mary F. H. and John DeBrot, are recorded as living in
St. Marys with their several children, including a girl
aged fifteen to twenty years, presumably the maker of
this sampler.

10

WASHSTAND

Savannah, Chatham County, or Effingham County, ca. 1830-1840
Made by John D. Wilkins (1808-1886)
Mahogany and mahogany veneers; yellow pine
35⅛ x 15⅞ x 15⅞ inches
Descent in family of maker
Lent by Mrs. Mary Webb Rabey
Color illustration on page 50

Although dozens of cabinetmakers are known to have worked in Savannah and coastal Georgia in the early nineteenth century, surviving examples of their work are scarce. John D. Wilkins is the only one of these early craftsmen for whom several pieces can be documented. This and another washstand, a drop-leaf work table, a chest of drawers with looking glass, a gentleman's dressing table, and a group of cabinet-maker's tools inscribed "W" have descended in Wilkins's family. The tools include glass and mold cutters, a bit brace, and two jack planes.

In both form and ornamentation, Wilkins's works are late expressions of the early nineteenth-century Federal style. The washstand and the chest of drawers with attached looking glass were new forms in that period. The turned legs on this washstand and the twisted rope turnings on the other are in the Federal style.

It is not known exactly when Wilkins arrived in Georgia or from where he came. In 1830 he married Rebecca Ann Lavender in Savannah. Nine years later, a widower, he married Mary Catherine Gnann, also in Savannah. (Both wives were Lutherans and direct descendants of the Salzburgers.) The 1850 Federal Census lists him in Effingham County with his wife, six children, and nine slaves; the 1860 Census describes him as a farmer in Effingham County, living with his wife and eleven children. According to family history, his home, known as Pineland, was at the seventeen-mile mark on the stagecoach road between Savannah and Louisville. After the Civil War, he moved back to Savannah, where he opened a shop and manufactured furniture at a location between Abercorn and Lincoln Streets.

11

SHELF CLOCK

Savannah, Chatham County, ca. 1840
Assembled by A. Sage and Company
Parts probably made in Connecticut
Mahogany; poplar and white pine; glass and metal
38¾ x 18 x 5½ inches
Label: "PATENT/EIGHT-DAY/BRASS CLOCKS,/
MADE AND SOLD BY A. SAGE & CO./WHOLE-
SALE AND RETAIL,/SAVANNAH, GEO./
WARRANTED IF WELL USED."
Lent by H. Paul Blatner Antiques, Savannah

The Savannah firm A. Sage and Company is known
by this and one other Empire-style clock but is not
mentioned in city directories or newspapers. Sage is
the sixth clockmaker known to have been assembling
and labeling shelf clocks like this one in Savannah.
The others are L. F. Hayden, H. A. Hill, M. & W.
Dyer, and C. B. Dibble—none of whom are recorded
as Savannah residents in the 1830 or 1840 Census.[1]

1. For further discussion of Georgia's early clockmakers,
   see G. Robert Coatney and Robert G. Scholtens,
   "Georgia-made Clocks," *Bulletin of The National
   Association of Watch and Clock Collectors*, 17 no. 5
   (October 1975): 471-77.

12

PAIR OF ANDIRONS

Savannah, Chatham County, ca. 1850
Attributed to Christian David LeBey, Jr. (1825-1870)
Brass and iron
23½ x 12½ x 24¾ inches
Descent in family of maker
Lent by Heath Laughlin, Jr.

These andirons and another set in the same family are
the only Georgia-made brass objects documented by
the Georgia Decorative Arts Survey. Both are attributed to Christian David LeBey, Jr., and are owned by
his descendants. According to family history, LeBey
operated a brass foundry in Savannah prior to the
Civil War; during the war, he cast cannon balls for the
Confederate army. His father Christian David LeBey
(1787-1827) had been a silversmith in Savannah. A
corner cupboard by his grandson, William Edward
LeBey, is included in this exhibition (no. 18).

The only other brass andirons attributed to a
Georgia maker are a pair in the collection of the
Museum of Early Southern Decorative Arts that were
found in Savannah and are dated around 1760. None
of the three sets have any maker's marks.

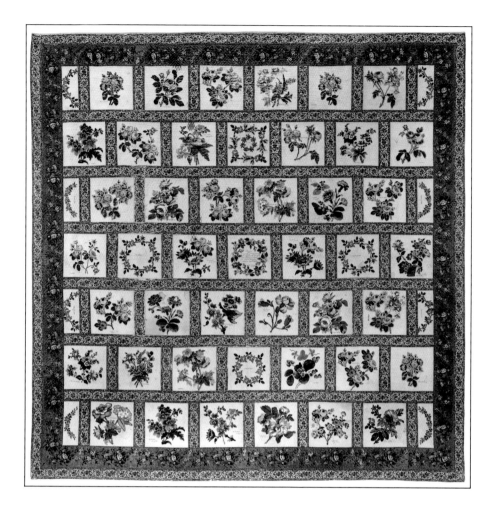

13

QUILT

Savannah, Chatham County, 1850
Made by members of the Second Baptist Church
Cotton
113 x 112 inches
Marks: "Presented/to/The Rev.d Henry O. Wyer &
lady/By their friends, the ladies of the/Second Baptist
Church/whose names are heron written/Savannah
May 1st 1850"; "John G. Holcombe/Scr"; and forty-
two signatures
The Telfair Academy of Arts and Sciences, Savannah,
gift of Mrs. Malcolm McLean, 1937

The Georgia Decorative Arts Survey identified many
album quilts made of appliquéd chintz (as in this
case), as well as geometric and floral pieced examples
made of printed calicoes. In general, the chintz quilts
are earlier and most include at least one signature
from Savannah.

The stacked and staggered arrangement of the
blocks on this album quilt is unusual, as is the wide
sashing of a different floral fabric. The quilt has forty-
five blocks, each of which has a distinctive bouquet or
stem of chintz flowers appliquéd with a buttonhole

stitch to the white background. On each block the
individual maker's name is signed in ink; some blocks
are also dated. The participants were members of the
Second Baptist Church and this quilt was made as
a special gift for the Reverend Henry O. Wyer and
his "lady."[1]

1. Within the presentation square is written "John G.
   Holcombe/Scr," which may identify Holcombe as the
   scribe who wrote the forty-two names: Charlotte M.
   Sweat, Ann A. Germain, E. T. Hilson, Caroline W.
   Lufburrow, Eugenia M. Winkler, Susan E. Simpson,
   C. Ellis, Agnes McIntosh, Jane R. Butler, E. L. Wilson,
   Margaret A. Stoney, Ann E. Brunner, Janet Winkler,
   Mary E. Smith, C. J. Cofre, Mary Lufburrow, C. M.
   Ellis, Sarah C. Olmstead, Mary C. File, Mary E. Webb,
   Georgia W. Olmstead, Sarah C. P. Postell, Abby Clark,
   Sarah G. Morrell, Sarah B. Clark, Mary Caroline Felt,
   Mrs. Jane Eliza Postell, A. L. Webb, Julia M. Tucker,
   Georgia A. R. Butler, A. Virginia Kempton, C. Johnson,
   Delia Ann Gardner, E. J. Winkler, Mary H. Dowell, Jane
   E. Postell, Jr., Eusebia E. Rabun, Caroline E. Overstreet,
   Ann C. Lendergreene, Jane R. Stilwell, Crawford Sutter,
   and Rebecca S. Norton.

Detail

14

QUILT

Savannah, Chatham County, ca. 1890
Made by Georgina Cohen Phillips (1841-1909)
Silk, satin, and velvet
78 x 73 inches
Descent in family of maker
The Juliette Gordon Low Girl Scout National
Center, Savannah
Color illustration on page 51

Georgina B. Cohen was born in Savannah in 1840
to Henryetta Y. and Octavus Cohen, a cotton factor.
Five brightly hued quilts of richly textured fabrics
have been attributed to her. These quilts were
inherited by two of her three daughters, Fanny and
Georgina Phillips, who were also quiltmakers. The
elder Georgina's quilts were bequeathed to the Juliette
Gordon Low House by the daughters, who had been
childhood friends of Juliette Gordon Low.

Georgina Phillips's quilt combines the geometric
order of mid-century pieced cotton quilts with the
richly textured fabrics and embroidery of later crazy
quilts. The center fabric, which resembles upholstery
material, is framed with a wide band of black velvet
embroidered with flowers. Brilliantly colored silk
crosses alternate with dark pieced polygons to form
the outer border. The piecing is worked with tiny,
almost invisible, stitches. The only quilt stitching out-
lines the leaf and flower motif on the blue silk border.

15

CARRIAGE OR CRIB QUILT

Savannah, Chatham County, 1883
Made by Sarah Davidson Cooper Nichols
(1860-1941)
Velvet and satin
28⅝ x 23½ inches
Descent in family of maker
Lent by Mrs. Alfred C. Nichols, Jr.

Burgundy velvet provides the background for a colorful bouquet of embroidered flowers, framed by a
border of quilted burgundy satin. This carriage quilt,
with its rich fabrics and elaborate flowers, is related
to crazy quilts of the period, but differs from them in
having one central embroidered design and no pieced
background. The asymmetry of the central motif was
perhaps inspired by Japanese designs, which influenced American decorative arts in the late nineteenth
century.

According to family history, this quilt was made for
the quilter's infant son, Alfred Cooper Nichols, born
in Savannah in 1883. Its small size suggests that it was
intended to be a carriage or crib quilt. Family members own other pieces of Sarah Nichols's handwork,
including a round drawn work tablecloth with
embroidery, embroidered napkins and place mats,
Battenburg lace table cloths, and several bedspreads.

16

GATE

Savannah, Chatham County, 1880-1907
Made by Kehoe and Company
Iron
42 x 29¾ inches
Mark: "KEHOE & CO MAKERS"
Lent by H. Paul Blatner Antiques, Savannah

From 1874 until 1877, William Kehoe was listed in
the Savannah city directories as a moulder, and then
in 1878 and 1879 as a foreman at the Phoenix Iron
Works. In 1880 the firm was listed as "William Kehoe
and Company, proprietors of Phoenix Iron Works,"
and in 1907 was incorporated as Kehoe Iron Works.

According to an advertisement in the 1881 City
Directory, the Phoenix foundry manufactured "iron
and brass castings, architectural iron work for
churches, stores, and dwellings; cemetery, verandah,
garden, and balcony railings; plow castings, etc.";
sugar mills and pans to be used in cane grinding were
a "specialty."

Kehoe was a civic leader in Savannah and Tybee. In
1893 he hired De Witt Bruyn to build a three-story
home of terra cotta brick and steel on Habersham
Street overlooking Columbia Square. Iron cast at the
Kehoe foundry was used for structural beams, window sills, outside steps, and ornate cornices over the
windows of the dwelling, which is still standing.

17

GRAVEMARKER

Probably Savannah, Chatham County, ca. 1915
Made by unknown artisan
Metals, celluloid, glass, and shells
12 x 4½ inches
Lent by H. Paul Blatner Antiques, Savannah

African-Americans living in coastal Georgia practiced funerary customs based on those of their
African ancestors. Imbedded in gravemarkers are
items probably belonging to the dead person, frag-
ments of everyday objects broken and tossed on the
grave, and items to be used in the afterlife. It was
believed that such gravemarkers would protect the
living relatives from being preyed upon by spirits of
the dead.[1]

This gravemarker reportedly came from the Woodville Cemetery, an African-American graveyard on
Fair Street in Savannah. It is a Holland gin bottle covered with clay, into which are stuck three cowry shells
(used as coins in African cultures), three machine-cut
nails, bits of colored glass, several buttons, a few
springs, a Frozen Charlotte doll (popular around
1890-1910), a tooth, a bell, a jack, a marble,
and a key.

1. See John Michael Vlach, *The African-American Tradition in Decorative Arts* (Cleveland: Cleveland Museum
of Art, 1978), pp. 144-47.

18

CORNER CUPBOARD

Savannah, Chatham County, 1893
Made by William Edward LeBey (1865-1959)
Walnut and birch; cypress
67¾ x 35½ inches
Marks: "Made by W. E. Lebey. 1893" on
plaque inside door
Descent in family of maker
Lent by Martha LeBey Lassiter
Color illustration on page 50

The Japanese pavillion at the 1876 Philadelphia Centennial Exposition helped spark American interest in Japanese arts and culture; American craftsmen responded by incorporating Japonesque motifs into furniture, ceramics, and textiles. William Edward LeBey, the maker of this cupboard, was clearly familiar with the Japanese-style marquetry used on fashionable Aesthetic Movement furniture of the 1880s. Inlaid on the sides and front of his cupboard are flowers and birds arranged in an asymmetrical, diagonal composition characteristic of that style.

On the inside of the cupboard door is a carved plaque in the shape of an eagle and shield; in the eagle's beak is a banner reading "Made by W. E. Lebey. 1893." Although this cupboard is the only large case piece known to have been made by LeBey, many smaller items by him survive, including an intricately carved cuckoo clock, calendars, and picture frames, all inlaid with a variety of woods.

LeBey, who worked in a Savannah hardware store and lumberyard, was the grandson of Christian David LeBey, Jr., to whom brass andirons in this exhibition are attributed (see no. 12).

THE COASTAL PLAIN REGION

The Coastal Plain region embraces more than half the land mass of Georgia. This relatively flat area is bounded on the north by the Fall Line running northeast to southwest, on the east by the Savannah River and the Tidewater region, on the south by Florida, and on the west by the Chattahoochee River, which separates Georgia from Alabama. Several of the state's major rivers flow through this region from their headwaters in the Piedmont to deltas in the Tidewater area; these include the Savannah, the Ogeechee, and the Oconee and Ocmulgee, which form the Altamaha. The Flint and the Chattahoochee rivers flow through the Coastal Plain into the Gulf of Mexico. In the nineteenth century, these rivers were important transportation routes for the region's trade.

The first white settlers in the region migrated north or west from the Tidewater area, and south from the Carolinas, Virginia, and other colonies. Beginning in the mid eighteenth century, they settled between the Savannah and the Ogeechee rivers. In the 1780s and 1790s, many Revolutionary War veterans came to claim land grants received for military service. The frontier pushed westward to the Oconee River. The first towns, isolated from one another in the region's pine barrens, included Waynesboro (founded in 1783) and Louisville (1796), which was the state capital until 1806. By the end of 1827 the Creek Indians had ceded all claims to lands in the region.

These newly opened lands were distributed by lottery to settlers venturing as far west as the Alabama border. Many new towns were settled during the first half of the nineteenth century, including Waycross (1825), Thomasville (1826), Americus (1832), and Albany (1836). The growth of these population centers, along with later towns such as Valdosta (1860) and Tifton (1872), was encouraged by the expansion of rail transportation during the mid and late nineteenth century.

During the survey, visits were made to many of the region's towns, including Louisville, Waynesboro, Tifton, Waycross, Valdosta, Thomasville, Moultrie, Albany, Americus, Statesboro, and Sandersville. A variety of furniture forms was found, with wardrobes, chairs, and tables the most numerous. Most of the furniture was made from native woods, primarily yellow pine and walnut; cherry and pecan were found in a few pieces in the western section. Some of this furniture retains its original painted or grained decoration in a variety of colors (see nos. 21 and 24). Unusual furniture forms from the region include a table (no. 19), a corner chair (no. 27), and a Japanese-style étagère (no. 39). Most of the richly-figured curly pine furniture documented for the survey was made in this area (see no. 36).

Many handmade bedcoverings were found in the Coastal Plain region. Documented textiles included an early appliquéd flower basket quilt (ca. 1830) attributed to a seventeen-year-old girl in Louisville (no. 22) and mid-century pieced block set quilts (nos. 25 and 32). Late nineteenth-century crazy quilts are rare in this region; one distinctive example was elaborately embroidered (no. 33). Knitted and crocheted bedspreads were apparently popular here and several were recorded (see nos. 40, 41, and 42). Although this area was a major sheep-raising region around the time of the Civil War, few wool textiles were found. However, the survey discovered one weaver who had made several coverlets which contained wool from black sheep raised on her family farm (no. 30).

Very few pieces of Georgia-made silver were documented in this region. Perhaps little was made here because flatware and hollow ware could easily be purchased from silversmiths, jewelers, and retailers in Augusta, Macon, Columbus, or Savannah. Most of the silver found here had the marks of Savannah silversmiths. An iron table base cast at the Pattison Foundry in Albany (no. 33) represents the region's late-nineteenth-century iron industry.

The Coastal Plain had one pottery site, in Lanier County. The families operating potteries there had migrated from South Carolina and middle Georgia, establishing businesses in the Coastal Plain by the late 1870s.[1] Their products were primarily utilitarian vessels, such as the Timmerman Jug Company's bowl (no. 38).

After the Civil War, the craft of china painting was promoted in the Coastal Plain region by William Lycett of Atlanta, who made annual winter trips to Albany to teach classes (no. 34). Decorating china was also a popular woman's activity in the Statesboro area.

1. Suzanne Harper et al., *Georgia Clay: Pottery of the Folk Tradition* (Macon: Museum of Arts and Sciences, 1989), p. 20.

19

TABLE

Probably Burke County, ca. 1800
Made by unknown artisan
Yellow pine and hickory; yellow pine
25 x 30 x 24½ inches
Descent in family of early owner
Private collection

Little is known about this early stretcher-based table. Its ownership can be traced back to Matthew W. Bunn (1825-1882) in Midville, Georgia. It has descended in Bunn's family along with a sideboard, a cupboard, and a bureau which were listed in his estate inventory and appraisement. Also recorded in this inventory was "1 lot of kitchen furniture" which may have included this table. A corner chair (no. 27), reportedly made for Bunn, is included in this exhibition.

Stretcher-based tables made in Georgia are very scarce. A mid-eighteenth-century example believed to have been made by a Salzburger craftsman in Ebenezer, Georgia, is in the collection of the Museum of Early Southern Decorative Arts.[1]

1. Another stretcher-based table is illustrated in Henry D. Green, *Furniture of the Georgia Piedmont before 1830* (Atlanta: High Museum of Art, 1976), p. 74.

20

ARMCHAIR

Bulloch County, ca. 1815-1851
Made by unknown artisan
Walnut with hide seat
40⅜ x 22¼ x 17½ inches
Descent in family of maker
Lent by Smith C. Banks

Samuel Alderman (1789-1851) moved from North Carolina to Bulloch County, Georgia, in 1815. Family history records that this chair is one of six made for him from walnut cut on the Alderman family property in Bulloch County. Also in the possession of the family is the Alderman cattle brand ("89," or possibly "68"), which appears on the original hide seat of a companion side chair.

Slat-back chairs were common in rural areas throughout the United States in the nineteenth century. Hide seats were often used in Georgia, especially in the middle and southern parts of the state.[1] The original hide seat, the use of walnut throughout the chair, the flattened ball finial above the attenuated neck, and the shape of the turned arm supports are noteworthy features of this armchair.

1. William W. Griffin et al., *Neat Pieces: The Plain-Style Furniture of 19th Century Georgia* (Atlanta: Atlanta Historical Society, 1983), p. 71.

21

DESK AND BOOKCASE

Fort Valley, Peach County, ca. 1840
Made by Alexander G. Slappey (1804-1884)
Yellow pine
79 x 45¼ x 29¼ inches
Descent in family of maker
Lent by Dr. and Mrs. J. Herbert West

Although it is believed that much early Georgia furniture was painted, especially the pine pieces, this desk is a rare surviving example of the practice. The mustard yellow paint is original to the piece.

The desk was made by Alexander Slappey, the third of nine children born to Polly Gordon and John George Slappey III in Edgefield County, South Carolina. Between 1810 and 1820, the Slappey family moved to a farm near Fort Valley in Crawford (now Peach) County in Georgia. As an adult, Alexander lived on a thousand-acre farm near Fort Valley; in 1871 he moved to Sumter County, where he spent the rest of his life. No other pieces of furniture are known to have been made by him.

22

QUILT

Louisville, Jefferson County, ca. 1830
Attributed to Philoclea Edgeworth Casey Eve
(1813-1889)
Cotton
90 x 102½ inches
Descent in family of maker
Private collection

During the period 1800-1840, roller-printed chintzes were made in six basic patterns: floral baskets and vases, trees, hunt cornucopia, pillar prints, rainbows, and commemoratives.[1] Quilters selected motifs, cut them out, and arranged unique compositions.

On this quilt, the maker chose a floral basket for the central design, surrounding it with several wreath-like borders and scattered bouquets. The background quilting, a running diamond stitch, was less skillfully worked than the appliqué stitching, and may be the work of another hand.

The quilt has descended in the Casey family, which attributes it to Philoclea Eve or to her mother, Sarah Lowndes Berrien Casey (1790-1822). The basket of flowers as a central medallion indicates a date around 1830.[2]

1. Florence M. Montgomery, *Printed Textiles: English and American Cottons and Linens, 1700-1850* (New York: Viking Press, 1970), pp. 343-59.
2. Dena S. Katzenberg, *Baltimore Album Quilts* (Baltimore: Baltimore Museum of Art, 1981), pp. 32, 63-65; and Ruth Haislip Roberson, ed., *North Carolina Quilts* (Chapel Hill, N. C.: University of North Carolina Press, 1988), pp. 43, 52.

SIDEBOARD OR SLAB

Washington County, ca. 1840
Made by unknown artisan
Yellow pine
51¾ x 39⅛ x 22¼ inches
Descent in family of early owner
Private collection

Popularly known today as "huntboards," small side-boards or slabs were popular in nineteenth-century Georgia. Many have been found but no two are identical.[1] On this example, traces of the original dark green paint highlight the molding of the plinths and splashboard, the front edge of the top surface, and the ring turnings on the legs. Turned legs are less common on Georgia sideboards than square, tapering ones.

Plinths and a splashboard are used occasionally on Georgia pieces (see nos. 56 and 101). The legs of this sideboard appear to have been shortened at the base.

According to a former owner, this sideboard was used by Martha Frances Giles Marsh (1879-1961) of Deepstep in Washington County until her death. Her descendants believe that she inherited it from her mother's family, the Jordans, also of Deepstep.

1. See Henry D. Green, *Furniture of the Georgia Piedmont before 1830* (Atlanta: High Museum of Art, 1976); and William W. Griffin et al., *Neat Pieces: The Plain-Style Furniture of 19th Century Georgia* (Atlanta: Atlanta Historical Society, 1983). For a discussion of nomenclature, see Griffin, p. 6.

24

CLOTHES PRESS

Probably Screven County, ca. 1836
Made by unknown artisan
Yellow pine
79 x 73 x 26¾ inches
Descent in family of original owner
Lent by Rabun A. (Alex) Lee, Jr.
Color illustration on page 53

Oyster white, dark green, and mustard yellow paints
were used to enhance the exterior of this yellow pine
clothes press. The interior was finished with a Spanish
brown wash. The survival of these original colors is
rare and noteworthy.

The diamond motif on these doors appeared
nowhere else in the survey. Other features of this press
were common to pieces of central Georgia furniture,
such as reeded moldings, inset paneled doors, and
bracket feet. The press is unusually wide, and the
scalloped skirt dips to the floor to serve as a middle
foot. There is no evidence that the piece ever had a
cornice. The interior of the press is divided into three
sections; the outer sections are fitted with shelves, and
the center section has six drawers and two shelves.

Family history reports that this clothes press was
made for Anna Brinson (1819-1903) and Simeon Burk
(1814-1887) around the time of their marriage in
1836. The family also owns a sideboard with similar
reeded moldings, made for the Burks at about the
same time.

25

QUILT

Perry, Houston County, ca. 1840
Made by Frances Sarah Anne Crocker Solomon
Dennard (1815-1886)
Cotton
73¼ x 73 inches
Label: "Mrs. H. L. Dennard" in ink
Descent in family of maker
Lent by Mr. and Mrs. William A. Fickling, Jr.
Color illustration on page 52

This colorful appliquéd quilt is one of two attributed
to Frances Sarah Anne Dennard. Both are designed
with large central patterns surrounded by several
borders, and both use the same fabrics and identical
quilt stitching. These quilts remained in the home of
Mrs. Dennard's daughter, Mary Frances Hughes,
until they were sold at Mrs. Hughes's estate sale in
1987, along with the contents of her Danville home,
Magnolia Plantation.

Detail

26

QUILT

Washington County, 1847-1852
Made by at least forty-one quilters
Cotton
98 x 96 inches
Marks: Signatures, towns, and work dates
of quilters in ink
Descent in family of original owner
Lent by Eugenia Selden Lehmann
Color illustration on page 55

The floral wreaths and bouquets of this album quilt
are separated by double rows of diagonal stitching.

At least five of the forty-one who signed this quilt
were men.[1] Seven were from Tidewater towns, twelve
from the Coastal Plain region, two from the Piedmont, and four from New Market, New Hampshire.
The common bond among the signees was probably
the Wadley family. William Morrill Wadley, formerly
of New Hampshire, married Rebecca B. Everingham
of Savannah in 1840. They lived first in Savannah,
then at Oakland, a plantation near Sandersville.
Wadley was the superintendent and later president
of the Central of Georgia Railroad, which linked
Savannah and Macon.

The quilt is believed to have been completed on
a plantation in the Macon area, either that of the
Wadley/Burt family or that of Anne Clark Tracy
Johnston (1829-1896), a cousin of the Wadleys.[2]

1. The legible names on the quilt are: Mary Ann Goodall,
   Mary F. Harman, James G. Neely, Samuel B. Crafton,
   M. B. Millen, Henrietta Lane Wadley, M. G. Solomon,
   Lou Goodall, D. R. Wadley, M. T. Charlton, H. R.
   Brown, C. M. Miller, Louisa B. Harman, C. F. Griffin,
   W. Holton, Mary Magdalene Dasher, Thomas L. Fulton,
   Henrietta Brown, Sarah Hadley, Caroline Tillson, C. D.
   McConnell, Elizabeth T. Smith, Jane Solomon, W. O.
   Charlton, Lydia C., M. E. Fulton, Martha S. Welch,
   L. W. Sofsolyn, Sarah L. Wadley, Sarah L. Wadley Burt,
   Rebecca D. Stanton, Mary Whitaker, Margaret Anna,
   Jacob P. Welch, Bennett Crafton, and William W. Holton.
2. Almost all the blocks are dated between 1847 and 1852.
   Two blocks are dated 1912, signed by Sarah L. Wadley
   (born 1844) and Sarah L. Wadley Burt, the daughter and
   granddaughter of Rebecca and William Wadley. Perhaps
   these blocks were signed later by these owners of the
   quilt, or perhaps they pieced and quilted the mid-century
   blocks in 1912. The fabric of the two later blocks
   matches that of the border.

Detail

27

CORNER CHAIR

Probably Burke County, ca. 1850
Made by unknown artisan
Unidentified woods with hide seat
28½ x 25¾ x 22¼ inches
Descent in family of original owner
Private collection

Although the corner chair was a popular form in
Europe and America in the eighteenth century,
it is extremely rare in Georgia. This is the only one
recorded in the Georgia Decorative Arts Survey.[1] This
hide is a replacement of the original hide seat.
    The chair descended in the Bunn family of Burke
County. It was reportedly made for Matthew W. Bunn
(1825-1882) of Midville (see no. 19).

1. Two references to corner chairs have been found in early
   nineteenth-century Hancock County inventories. See
   William W. Griffin et al., *Neat Pieces: The Plain-Style
   Furniture of 19th Century Georgia* (Atlanta: Atlanta
   Historical Society, 1983), p. 71.

28

ROCKING CHAIR

Stewart or Schley County, ca. 1850
Made by unknown artisan
Hickory with hide seat
41¼ x 20½ x 14½ inches
Marks: "TB" incised on back of slat
Descent in family of early owner
Lent by Charles R. Crisp

This rocking chair has pointed finials, shaped slats,
and scored back posts—features similar to those on
a set of chairs made in 1856 for the Chattahoochee
County Courthouse in Cusseta and attributed to
Perry Spencer of Stewart County.[1] Both the rocker and
the courthouse chairs are made of hickory, but the
posts of the rocking chair are more deeply turned.
The chair's original owner, Robert Burton, lived in
Ellaville, a town in Schley County, not far from
Stewart County.

1. William W. Griffin et al., *Neat Pieces: The Plain-Style
   Furniture of 19th Century Georgia* (Atlanta: Atlanta
   Historical Society, 1983), p. 83.

29

SIDEBOARD

Kingfisher Plantation, Quitman, Brooks County,
probably before 1852
Made by unknown artisan
Cherry; yellow pine
43¼ x 61⅛ x 22⅝ inches
Marks: "1851" incised; "the 22 Sept I may take
out/ my oil st————" in ink inside drawer
Descent in family of original owner
Private collection

According to family tradition, this sideboard was
made by slaves on Kingfisher Plantation, the Quitman
property of James Everett Young and Lavinia Young
Young.[1] The incised date in a top drawer suggests that
the sideboard was made by 1851.

Sideboards were introduced into America as a new
furniture form in the late eighteenth century. In the
nineteenth century, urban sideboards became
increasingly large, heavy, and ornate. This rural
example reflects the early Federal style, with a less
imposing linear design, and drawers and cupboards
designed for various uses. In this instance, the side

drawers are very narrow. The use of cherry as the primary wood is unusual for a piece made in southern
Georgia; cherry is more common in the mountainous
northern part of the state.

A bookcase owned by James Young's brother-in-law, Archibald Thomas MacIntyre, is also in this
exhibition (see no. 36).

1. Plantation papers, now a part of the Belle Young Collection at the Lowndes County Historical Society, list no
slaves trained in cabinetmaking. The papers do include
some records of the sale of slaves, citing the slaves by
name, reporting the prices paid for them, and giving
brief physical descriptions along with mention of their
specialized skills.

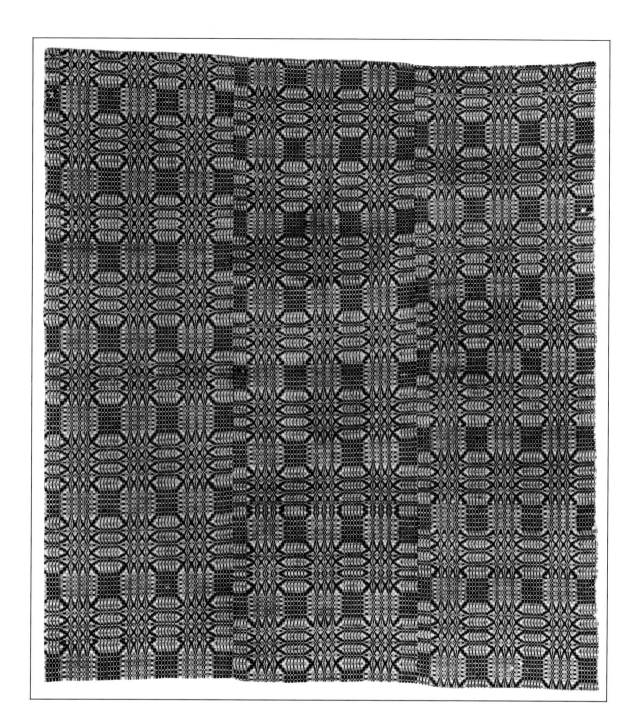

30

COVERLET

Sylvester, Worth County, ca. 1860
Made by Charlotte Burch Sikes (1824-1903)
Wool and cotton
87 x 81 inches
Descent in family of maker
Lent by Joe F. and Margaret S. Lawson, Jr.

This three-piece overshot coverlet is woven in a variation of the Pine Cone Bloom pattern, using black wool and natural unbleached cotton. The wool for the weft was sheared from black sheep raised on the family farm, then carded and spun by Charlotte. Several of the coverlets she wove for her family survive; two of them and a smaller lap robe also use black wool.

Charlotte Burch Sikes was the daughter of Sarah and Benjamin Burch. In 1861 or 1862, she married Judge Eli Sikes. They lived on a large farm where Judge Sikes raised sheep.

31

WARDROBE

Leslie, Sumter County, ca. 1866
Made by James J. Harp (1842-1920)
Yellow pine
81½ x 57⅝ x 21½ inches
Descent in family of maker
Private collection
Color illustration on page 54

The distinctive features of this wardrobe are the recessed front panels with their beveled-edge scalloped framing and applied ring-turned split spindle decoration—elaborate details which are seldom seen

on Georgia-made furniture.

In its other details, this wardrobe is typical of Georgia furniture of the period; it has a wide flaring cornice, simple upper moldings, and uses one board to form the scalloped skirt and feet. The sides of the wardrobe are formed of single boards with a Gothic arch at the base. Traces of white paint in the joints indicate that the yellow pine exterior was once painted.

According to family history, this case piece was made after Harp returned from the Civil War, perhaps around the time of his marriage to Mary Elizabeth Bass in 1866.

32

QUILT

Blackshear, Pierce County, ca. 1860
Attributed to Jane Albritton Jones Stephens
(1830s-1912)
Cotton
75 x 64 inches
Descent in family of maker
Lent by Mr. and Mrs. Kendall Zeliff

The abstract Rose of Sharon pattern on this quilt is made up of several layers of cotton rather than the customary single layer. The appliquéd floral motifs are further accentuated by tight background quilting in the shell pattern.

The composition and coloration of this quilt suggest a date between 1850 and 1870. The grid dividing the four large blocks became an increasingly popular feature by mid-century, gradually replacing central medallion patterns. The solid colors–chrome yellow, green, and reddish brown–came into common use in the 1850s; by the 1870s, the chrome yellow, a synthetic dye, was discontinued.

This is one of several quilts that a descendant found in a family chest containing the belongings of Sarah Jane Jones Brown (1855-1938). This quilt was attributed to her because she was remembered as an avid needleworker. However, the dates of the dyes and the style of the quilt indicate a date prior to 1870, suggesting that Sarah's mother, Jane Albritton Jones Stephens, is more likely to have been the quilter.

33

TABLE

Albany, Dougherty County, ca. 1870s-1900
Attributed to Thomas Pattison and Sons Foundry
and Machine Shop
Iron and walnut
28⅝ x 31⅛ x 25⅜ inches
Descent in Pattison family
Private collection

Although a number of foundries were active in the state in the nineteenth century, iron furniture known to have been made in Georgia is uncommon. This table, which descended in the Pattison family, may have been made at the Thomas Pattison and Sons Foundry and Machine Shop, which opened at Washington and Flint Streets in Albany in the 1870s. Pattison, a native of Yorkshire, England, had lived in New York City, Chattanooga, and Decatur, Alabama, before settling in Albany.

In a will written in 1896, Pattison bequeathed his "foundry lots with all the foundry equipment of all kinds" to his sons Richard and Samuel and his grandson Richard Thomas. Two other sons, John and Thomas, were working at the foundry when it closed after their father's death in 1898.

Cast iron furniture became popular in America in the 1840s, particularly for garden use. Scrolls and nature motifs in the rococo-revival style were introduced then and remained in vogue for decades.

34

TUREEN AND BOWLS

Albany, Dougherty County, 1888
Painted by Sarah Augusta Tucker Muse (1862-1922)
Porcelain
Tureen: 6½ x 13 x 8 inches; bowl: 7⅜ inches wide
Marks: "Sallie Tucker" painted on underside of each piece; "SAT" and "1888" painted on lid of tureen; "H & Co./L" stamped on underside of each piece
Descent in family of painter
Lent by Leigh W. Brooks

This soup tureen and twelve bowls are part of a large dinner service decorated with marine and nautical motifs by Sarah Augusta Tucker Muse. Her descendants believe that she did this work under the direction of William Lycett, the renowned china painter from Atlanta, who conducted china painting classes in Albany each January and February. The classes used undecorated porcelain manufactured in Europe.

Sarah Augusta Tucker Muse was the daughter of Mr. and Mrs. Jesse Tucker of Lee County. She painted the service in the year preceding her marriage to Augustus Winn Muse, Sr., of Albany. In addition to her china painting, Sallie Tucker Muse was active in Albany organizations throughout her life, including the Thronateeska Chapter of the National Society of the Daughters of the American Revolution, the Albany Women's Club, the Chautauqua Literary and Scientific Circle, the Albany Methodist Church, and the Parsonage Aid Society.

35

QUILT

Thomasville, Thomas County, ca. 1890
Made by Sarah A. Davis Peters (1841-ca. 1910)
Wool, velvet, silk, and satin
63³/4 x 63³/4 inches
Thomas County Historical Society, Inc., Thomasville

Sarah Peters, like many late nineteenth-century quilters, selected fabrics, motifs, and compositions quite freely. Here she embellished the sixteen blocks of her quilt with flowers, birds, butterflies, pears, and tennis racquets. The pears refer to the LeConte pear, one of Thomasville's major crops in the 1880s; the tennis racquets refer to Thomasville's post-Civil War

popularity as a winter resort. The town had two major resort hotels and a number of private rental cottages, and offered lawn tennis and golf. Joseph C. Peters, Sarah's husband, built the Waverly Hotel in Thomasville in 1881; after his death, Sarah continued to own it until 1887.

The stitching on this quilt is the work of an accomplished needleworker. In fact, according to the 1880 Census, Sarah Peters was a milliner. On this quilt she extended elaborate embroidery beyond the sixteen blocks, using a variety of delicate stitches to join the blocks to the wide velvet border and adding a floral vine to the border itself.

36

BOOKCASE

Thomasville, Thomas County, ca. 1890
Made by Reynolds, Hargrave and Sons Variety Works
or Edward Orlando Thompson Variety Works
Yellow pine
95½ x 71½ x 20 inches
Descent in family of original owner
Lent by Mrs. Thomas T. Hawkins

This and three similar curly pine bookcases were made for the law office of Archibald Thomas MacIntyre, Sr. (1822-1900), a member of the 1847-1848 State Legislature, a trustee of the University of Georgia, and a trustee of the state asylum.[1] The bookcases were made by one of the two Variety Works operating in Thomasville in 1889—the Reynolds, Hargrave and Sons Variety Works or the Edward Orlando Thompson Variety Works. Both made and sold fine millwork, including mantles, scrollwork, balusters, stair rails, newel posts, and blinds.[2] It is not known which firm made these bookcases.

The four bookcases were treated with a dark stain to imitate the rich grains of burled walnut, crotch mahogany, or bird's eye maple.[3]

1. Archibald Thomas MacIntyre's brother-in-law owned a sideboard which is in this exhibition (see no. 27).
2. William R. Mitchell, Jr., *Landmarks: The Architecture of Thomasville and Thomas County, Georgia, 1820-1920* (Thomasville, Ga.: Thomasville Landmarks, 1980), p. 128.
3. The January 24, 1880, *Brunswick Advertiser* mentions the dark staining of curly pine.

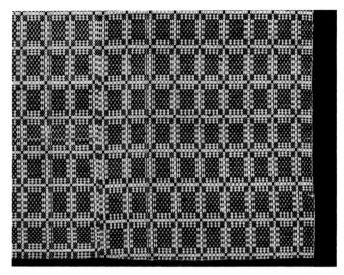

Detail

37

COVERLET

Claxton, Evans County, ca. 1880
Made by Elizabeth Smart Grice Durrence
(1838-1922)
Wool and cotton
91¾ x 82 inches
Descent in family of maker
Lent by Dorothy Durrence Simmons

This three-section overshot coverlet was woven in a variation of the Patch pattern. It has an unbleached cotton warp (vertical threads) and a weft (horizontal threads) of hand-dyed and spun black and red wools. The cotton gave strength to the coverlet while the wool provided warmth.

The coverlet is one of a group of at least nine known to have been made by Elizabeth Smart Grice Durrence. The wool and cotton she used in her coverlets were produced on her family farm, settled around 1800 by her grandfather and still owned by her family.

According to family history, Elizabeth Durrence was a prolific weaver. She made this coverlet for her oldest child, Hartridge Jerome Durrence (1859-1897), around the time of his marriage to Mary Ann Rogers. Other surviving coverlets made by her include one of brown and beige wool, and one of blue and yellow wool. The three coverlets display different weaving patterns. The cards, counter, and spinning wheel used by Mrs. Durrence are still owned by family members; her loom hung in the barn until it disintegrated.

Elizabeth Durrence took up quilting later in life. Only one of her quilts survives—a black and white calico with black stars. Pieced by her in 1913 and quilted by her daughter, Neva Durrence, it is now owned by the Claxton Library.

38

BOWL

Stockton, Lanier County, ca. 1900
Made by Timmerman Jug Company
Stoneware with alkaline glaze
3½ x 8¼ inches
Marks: "T" stamped on base
Private collection

This small round bowl is typical of the utilitarian pottery made in Georgia during the second half of the nineteenth century. Gray or tan clays were used to make the hard and dense stoneware body; the alkaline glaze was made of ground ash or lime, clay, and sand mixed with water.

Most of Georgia's nineteenth-century pottery centers were located in the Piedmont region or along the Fall Line, where the necessary fine clays were available. One of the few pottery centers outside that region was Stockton in Clinch (now Lanier) County, which had three family-run concerns at the end of the century—potteries operated by the Timmermans, the Foremans, and the Fenders.

Little is known of the Timmerman potters or their work.[1] The Timmerman Jug Company was probably founded by the sons of Shimuel Timmerman (1824-1889), a farmer who migrated to Clinch County by 1850 from Edgefield County, South Carolina, a major pottery center. Clinch County deed books tell us only that "The Timmerman Jug Company" acquired seventeen acres of land in 1903, selling it again in 1905. The 1900 Census identifies Shimuel's ten children as farmers and merchants, with no mention of the pottery.

1. The mark "T" has been identified as that of the Timmerman Jug Company by Jerry Schmidt in the exhibition catalogue *Georgia Clay* (Macon, Ga.: Museum of Arts and Sciences, 1989), p. 20.

39

Etagère

Americus, Sumter County, 1892
Made by James Wilson Harris (1839-1924)
Walnut and poplar; white pine; brass
70³/₄ x 48 x 13 inches
Marks: "J W Harris/Americus Ga/PRINTED/Dec 23/
1892" in pencil inside on back of compartment;
"Shelton Harris" in pencil on side of compartment
Descent in family of maker
Lent by Mr. and Mrs. Charles K. Johnston

James Wilson Harris, the owner of Harris's Hardware
Store in Americus, was familiar with the Japanese
fashion popular in America in the late nineteenth century (see no. 18). Far Eastern influence can be seen on
the pagoda-like crest of his étagère, the spindle fans,

the low-relief carving on the compartment door, and
the faux bamboo finish. His granddaughter recalls
shipments of white pine boards being unloaded from
the train for delivery to the hardware store. Shelton
Harris, whose name is inscribed on the side of the
compartment, was the son of J. W. Harris.

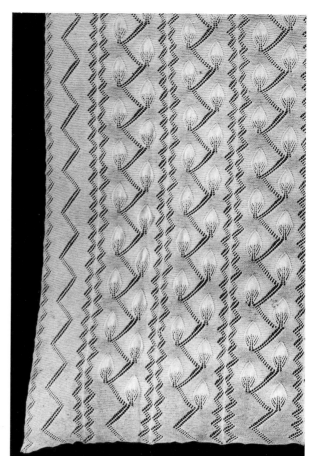

Detail

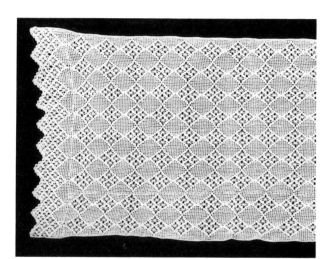

Detail

40

Sham

Centerville, Houston County, ca. 1890
Made by Sarah Elizabeth Hardison Tucker
(1867-1946)
Cotton
22¼ x 88 inches
Descent in family of maker
Lent by Mrs. Nell Tucker Popper

This pillow sham and a matching bedspread were
crocheted by Sarah Elizabeth Hardison Tucker. Using
fine cotton threads, she produced an unusually delicate small-scale diamond pattern. The same pattern
was worked on a larger scale by Annie Lewis Rushin
Willingham of Macon at about the same time
(see no. 90.)

Very little is known about Sarah Tucker. The
daughter of Mr. and Mrs. Allen Hardison, she married George Daniel Tucker in 1886. They lived on a
farm in Centerville. No other pieces by Sarah Tucker
have survived.

41

Bedspread

Plains, Sumter County, ca. 1890
Made by Laura Rachel Addy Wise (1864-1964)
Cotton
86 x 85 inches
Descent in family of maker
Lent by Louise Wise Teaford

This Leaves and Zigzag counterpane or bedspread
followed a pattern popularized in Butterick's *Fancy
and Practical Knitting*. This motif for the intermedi-
ate knitter used the stockinette stitch in the leaf
pattern and a garter stitch background, forming the
zigzag design.[1]

The Georgia Decorative Arts Survey documented
approximately one hundred knitted or crocheted bedspreads. The majority were made around 1900. Many
patterns were used, especially stars and flowers. Some
patterns, like this one, were worked to have a flat surface; others were highly textured. All were worked
with cotton yarn.

1. Mary Walker Phillips, *Knitting Counterpanes: Traditional Coverlet Patterns for Contemporary Knitters*
(Newtown, Conn.: Taunton Press, 1989), pp. 4, 16.

42

BEDSPREAD

Tennille, Washington County, ca. 1900
Attributed to Melissa Veal Boatright (1845-1932)
Cotton
82 x 80½ inches
Descent in family of maker
Lent by Sara Mathis Chambers

This bedspread was knitted in the Star Tidy pattern,
which was popular in the late nineteenth century.
Knit and purl stitches were combined to create a flat
surface. The 120 knitted blocks were joined by
crocheted stitches and framed by a crocheted zigzag
scalloped border.

The spread descended in the family of Melissa
Boatright and is attributed to her because she is
remembered as regularly doing handwork. The
family owns other pieces believed to be her work,
including quilts and crocheted and knitted pillow
shams. The daughter of Sara Hall and John T. Veal
of Washington County, Melissa married Captain
Benjamin Sessions Boatright in 1866.

43

DESK

Blackshear, Pierce County, ca. 1915
Made by Everett Riley Jones (1885-1955)
Cedar
37 x 39 x 26½ inches
Lent by Blackshear Presbyterian Church

An unpublished ledger book containing the history
of Blackshear Presbyterian Church, including parish
marriages, deaths, and communions, records brief
statements about the building of the church in 1901.
A post-dated entry describes the history of the desk:
"The beautiful cedar trees that for so many years
adorned the church yard were planted by Mrs. Janet
B. Brantley and Mrs. Henry J. Smith. It became neces-
sary to cut down a number of them in recent years.
Mr. Edgar Leroy Pitman cured the wood and had
Mr. Everett Jones make the beautiful desk now in the
Bible classroom. The collection box and map pointer
also made of this cedar wood, is the work of Mr.
Jones' son, Thomas."[1]

Everett Riley Jones was born in Hoboken, Brantley
County, in 1885. He apparently learned cabinetmaking from his father, James A. Jones, and began making
furniture at home. By 1926, he had opened a cabinetmaking shop, working with his son Thomas.

1. Unpublished ledger, "History of Blackshear Church,"
   pp. JJ-M.

Quilt, Savannah, Chatham County, before 1821, made by Ann Legardere Clay, High Museum of Art, gift of Helen Stiles Rose, cat. no. 5.

Sampler, Savannah, Chatham County, 1824, made by Mary Elizabeth Vallotton Wells, lent by Anne Brooks Bazemore, cat. no. 7.

Washstand, Savannah, Chatham County, or Effingham County, ca. 1830-1840, made by John D. Wilkins, lent by Mrs. Mary Webb Rabey, cat. no. 10.

Corner Cupboard, Savannah, Chatham County, 1893, made by William Edward LeBey, lent by Martha LeBey Lassiter, cat. no. 18.

Quilt, Savannah, Chatham County, ca. 1890, made
by Georgina Cohen Phillips, The Juliette Gordon Low
Girl Scout National Center, Savannah, cat. no. 14.

COASTAL PLAIN

Quilt, Perry, Twiggs County, ca. 1840, made by
Frances Sarah Anne Crocker Solomon Dennard, lent
by Mr. and Mrs. William A. Fickling, Jr., cat. no. 25.

Clothes Press, probably Screven County, ca. 1836, made by unknown artisan, lent by Rabun A. (Alex) Lee, Jr., cat. no. 24.

Wardrobe, Leslie, Sumter County, ca. 1866, made by
James J. Harp, private collection, cat. no 31.

Quilt, Washington County, 1847-1852, made by at least forty-one quilters, lent by Eugenia Selden Lehmann, cat. no. 26.

Blanket Chest, possibly DeKalb County, ca. 1825,
made by unknown artisan, private collection,
cat. no. 51.

Blanket Chest, Walton County, ca. 1840, made by
unknown artisan, private collection, cat. no. 52.

Quilt, Oglethorpe County, 1835, made by Charlotta
Barnett Hardman, lent by Mary Sue Jones Barron,
cat. no. 53.

Corner Cupboard, Wilkes or Oglethorpe County, before 1836, made by unknown artisan, lent by Mr. and Mrs. Roger Bregenzer, cat. no. 49.

Quilt, detail, Sunnyside, Spalding County, ca. 1870, made by Mary Elizabeth Manley Malaier, lent by Ava Malaier Hill, cat. no. 75.

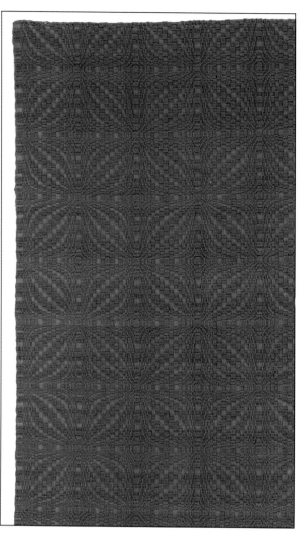

Coverlet, detail, Newtown, Madison County, ca. 1840, attributed to Elizabeth David, lent by Mrs. Roper Bell David, Sr., cat. no. 55.

Jewelry Box, Augusta, Richmond County, ca. 1860-1881, made by Charles A. Ladeveze, private collection, cat. no. 72.

Sideboard, Lincolnton, Lincoln County,
ca. 1894-1910, made by Harold Charles "Chick"
Harris, lent by Isabelle C. Pitts, cat. no. 84.

Quilt, detail, Atlanta, Fulton County, ca. 1880-1900, made by Margaret Josephine VanDyke Inman, lent by William Edward Rudolph, cat. no. 78.

Vase, Stevens Pottery, Baldwin County, ca. 1876-1900, made by Stevens Brothers & Company, lent by Mr. and Mrs. William A. Fickling, Jr., cat. no. 76.

Quilt, detail, Dallas, Paulding County, 1897, made by Narcissa Caroline Woodall Pearson, Ada Mae Pearson, and Georgia Ellen Pearson, private collection, cat. no. 85.

Quilt, Cumming, Forsyth County, 1837, made by
Nancy P. Holbrook Tribble, lent by Robert B. and
Winnie Tallant, cat. no. 96.

Bookcase, Sonoraville, Gordon County, ca. 1877, made by John Yule McEntyre, private collection, cat. no. 105.

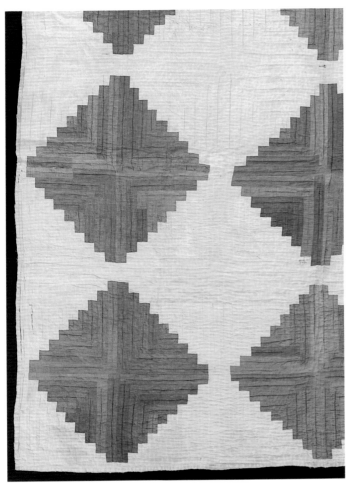

Quilt, detail, Rome, Floyd County, ca. 1915, made by
students at The Berry School, The Martha Berry
Museum of Berry College, Rome, cat. no. 108.

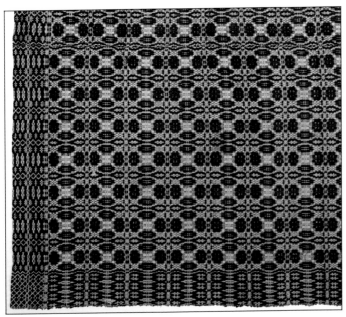

Coverlet, detail, Tallulah Falls, Habersham County,
ca. 1915, made by students at Tallulah Falls Industrial
School, Tallulah Falls School, cat. no. 109.

THE PIEDMONT REGION

This region of gently rolling hills and valleys, between the Highlands on the north and the Coastal Plain on the south, comprises about thirty percent of Georgia. The Fall Line is the geographic demarcation between the higher elevations and clay soils of this region and the sandy Coastal Plain. The headwaters of the Oconee and Ocmulgee Rivers are here, and the Savannah and Chattahoochee rivers flow through the region; these rivers served as transportation arteries for the Fall Line towns of Augusta, Milledgeville, Macon, and Columbus.

The earliest town in the Piedmont is Augusta, settled by the English in 1736 as a fort and trading post on the Savannah River. Following the Revolution, settlers, many of Scots-Irish and German descent, followed the Philadelphia Wagon Road and other trails into Georgia. They settled former Indian lands as far west as the Oconee River and north of Augusta to the mountains, establishing the towns of Wrightsboro, Washington, Elberton, and Greensboro in the eighteenth century. Athens (1801) grew up around Franklin College (later the University of Georgia), which had been chartered in 1785. In the nineteenth century, Macon (1823), Columbus (1828), and Atlanta (1837) were established. As the population moved inland, Georgia's political capital shifted also, to the Piedmont towns of Milledgeville in 1806 and Atlanta in 1868. Atlanta, originally called Terminus, traces its beginnings to the Zero Milepost staked for the southern end of the Western and Atlantic Railroad. The major cities of the region had access to river and later rail transportation linking them to one another, to the coastal ports, and to the smaller towns of the region.

By the time of the Civil War, more than half of the state's population lived in the Piedmont. More than half of the Georgia-made artifacts found by the survey were in this region, in Augusta, Athens, Milledgeville, Madison, Macon, Griffin, Columbus, Atlanta, and LaGrange. These artifacts survived in spite of the destruction of many of the region's

towns, farms, and plantations during the Civil War. Sherman's march to the sea destroyed much of the Atlanta-Macon corridor; an explosion in an ammunition depot decimated part of downtown Augusta; and, a week after the war officially ended, General James Wilson and his Union raiders set Columbus ablaze. Undoubtedly, many of the region's artifacts did not survive the war.

The number of objects in this exhibition is in proportion to the findings of the survey: more than half are from the Piedmont region, with furniture and textiles the largest categories. Furniture documented in the region tends to be conservative in style and similar to examples published in earlier studies.[1] These newly identified pieces, along with information about their makers and early owners, help to confirm the dates and local provenance of some previously published pieces. Native walnut and yellow pine were the most commonly used primary woods, with yellow pine and poplar the favored secondary woods. The survey found some furniture made of imported mahogany (see no. 56) and a few examples of curly pine from areas near the Savannah River (nos. 82 and 84). The mahogany and curly pine pieces were more decorative than the other Piedmont furniture. A variety of distinctive painted and grained surfaces were also found (nos. 49, 51, 52, 59, and 63).

Many handmade bedcoverings have survived in this region, including pieced and appliquéd quilts, woven wool and cotton coverlets, and knitted and crocheted cotton bedspreads. The fabrics included cottons and wools produced at home, woven cotton from local factories, and printed chintzes, calicos, silks, velvets and satins from the North and abroad.

Metalwares found in the Piedmont include silver, pewter, and iron. The silver bears the marks of both silversmiths and silver retailers doing business in the larger cities and towns. Silver flatware with family histories in the area was found in large quantities, evidence of the region's prosperity; yet there is a puzzling lack of hollow ware. Unusual pieces of silver found in the Piedmont include a covered bowl and salver from Augusta (no. 60), and a set of thirty-six goblets engraved in Macon (no. 71). Pewter tableware is very scarce—only three pieces of Georgia-made pewter are known; one was discovered during this survey (no. 45).

The fine clays of the Piedmont region encouraged potting families to establish their manufactories in Barrow, Fulton, Pike, and Upson counties (as well as Crawford County, which straddles the Fall Line). The potteries produced both alkaline-glazed stonewares for home use (jugs, churns, bowls, crocks) and unglazed pieces (whiskey jugs used by the local distilleries, garden kerbs, and gravemarkers).[2] Stevens Brothers and Company, originally located at Stevens Pottery, south of Milledgeville, is the only Georgia pottery known to have used a mottled yellow and brown lead glaze, often described as "Rockingham" (no. 76).

Classes in china painting were taught in the Piedmont as private businesses, like the Lycett studio in Atlanta, or as part of the curriculum at girls schools such as Lucy Cobb Institute in Athens and Cox College in Manchester (now College Park).

1. See Henry D. Green, *Furniture of the Georgia Piedmont before 1830* (Atlanta: High Museum of Art, 1976) and William W. Griffin et al., *Neat Pieces: The Plain-Style Furniture of Nineteenth Century Georgia* (Atlanta: Atlanta Historical Society, 1983).
2. John Burrison, *Brothers in Clay: The Story of Georgia Folk Pottery* (Athens: University of Georgia Press, 1983), p. 163 ff.

44

TABLE

Winfield, Columbia County, ca. 1810
Made by Basil O'Neal (1758-1849)
Walnut
30 x 50¼ x 19 inches
Descent in family of maker
Lent by Ruth Mayo

This table is one of a group of similar tables which have close ties to Columbia and McDuffie Counties. All of these tables have square tapered legs and applied molding under the top and along the skirt. (On one of these tables, the molding extends higher and may have originally enclosed a marble inset top.)

This is the only table of the group which has a known maker. Basil O'Neal, a native of Maryland, was an early settler of Columbia County, arriving there before or during the American Revolution. Along with a corner cupboard by the same maker, this piece descended in the O'Neal family.

45

PLATE

Augusta, Richmond County, before 1817
Attributed to Thomas Danforth IV (1792-1836)
Pewter
7¾ inches in diameter
Marks: Eagle with shield and stars stamped
on reverse
Descent in family of original owner
Private collection

When this plate was made, it was a common household item; today, it is surprisingly rare—one of only three recorded pieces of early Georgia-made pewter. The maker, Thomas Danforth IV, was the fourth generation of a family of pewterers who had practiced their craft in New England and Philadelphia. Thomas moved to Augusta, Georgia, from Philadelphia. Three other pewterers from New England were working in Augusta at the same time: Giles Griswold, 1818-1823; John North, 1818-1824; and Adna S. Rowe, 1818-1828.[1]

According to family tradition, this plate was purchased from Danforth by George Harris, a farmer living in Warren County, about forty miles west of Augusta. Harris died in 1817. The inventory and appraisal of his estate, recorded in 1821, listed:

5 pewter dishes	$10.00
5 pewter basons	5.00
21 pewter plates	5.00

Along with real estate totaling 1442 acres, the inventory included four slaves, livestock, farm equipment, and a long list of furnishings.

1. The Henry Francis du Pont Winterthur Museum owns two plates (with incomplete marks), one attributed to North and Rowe, the other to Griswold.

46

SPECTACLES

Eatonton, Putnam County, ca. 1821
Made by Daniel Booth Hempsted (1784-1852)
Silver
4½ inches wide
Marks: "D. B. HEMPSTED." stamped on both arms
Private collection

Although much silver flatware with Georgia hallmarks was found during the Georgia Decorative Arts Survey, this is the only pair of spectacles seen. Daniel Hempsted trained and worked as a watchmaker. He was recorded as working in Georgia only in 1821.[1] That same year he was also recorded as working in New London, Connecticut.[2]

1. George Barton Cutten, *The Silversmiths of Georgia* (Savannah, Ga.: Pigeonhole Press, 1958), p. 49.
2. Ralph M. Kovel and Terry H. Kovel, *A Directory of American Silver, Pewter and Silver Plate* (New York: Crown Publishers, Inc., 1961), p. 135.

47

CLOTHES PRESS

Jackson County, ca. 1830
Made by unknown artisan
Tulip poplar; yellow pine
87³/₄ x 44 x 22¹/₂ inches
Descent in family of early owner
High Museum of Art, purchase with funds from the
Decorative Arts Endowment

A common form in the South, the clothes press was
used to store clothes that were laid flat rather than
hung. On this example, the upper section, the cupboard, is fitted with one shelf; the lower section has

four drawers.

This press has several features in common with
other Piedmont furniture: the cavetto molded cornice,
the dentil molding, and the bracket feet. Four of the
original pressed lead glass knobs (probably from
New England or the Philadelphia area) remain on the
top two drawers of the case; one knob has leather
washers that may be original on both the exterior and
interior of the drawer.

The clothes press descended in the Freeman family,
whose ancestors settled in Franklin (later Jackson)
County as early as 1800.

48

Corner Cupboard

Hall or Jackson County, ca. 1820
Made by unknown artisan
Walnut; yellow pine
88 x 53½ inches
Descent in family of original owner
Private collection

The most striking feature of this corner cupboard is the scalloping which frames the eight tall panels of the doors. Similar scalloping was found on one other piece from this area, a small walnut spice chest, ca. 1820, reportedly from Oglethorpe County. This corner cupboard also has reeded blocks on the frieze, a classical detail. On the interior, the upper section has three stationary shelves, and the lower section one. There is no evidence that the piece ever had a cornice.

According to family tradition, the cupboard first belonged to a Mr. Bridges, who worked at Tanner's Grist Mill, built before 1820 on the Middle Oconee River in Hall County.

49

CORNER CUPBOARD

Wilkes or Oglethorpe County, before 1836
Made by unknown artisan
Yellow pine
87¼ x 47½ inches
Descent in family of early owner
Lent by Mr. and Mrs. Roger Bregenzer
Color illustration on page 58

An unusual feature of this corner cupboard is the scalloped fascia board just below the interior cornice. Other decorative additions include the crisply executed dentil molding, the beveled edges of the inner door frames, and the Prussian blue paint on the case. The machine-cut nails used in making this piece are of two types: those with hand-hammered heads and those with machine-hammered heads.

Until recently this cupboard descended in the family of John Eidson (ca. 1762-1815) of Wilkes County. Originally from North Carolina, Eidson was listed in a Wilkes County militia district by 1793. According to family history, his son Joseph Eidson (1804-1877) moved to Oglethorpe County in the 1830s, and to a farm in Palmetto in Campbell (now Fulton) County around 1836.

50

WORK TABLE

Banks County, ca. 1825
Made by unknown artisan
Walnut; yellow pine
29½ x 30½ x 23½ inches
Marks: Illegible chalk inscription on side of drawer
Descent in family of maker
Lent by Mr. and Mrs. William W. Griffin

The inlaid bellflower and stringing—as well as the dimensions, materials, and construction—relate this table to several others that have been found in the Piedmont region of Georgia.[1] This table differs, however, in having two upper drawers rather than one, and in having a history of continuous ownership in one Georgia Piedmont family. Also, because this table has never been restored, the authenticity of the

inlaid decoration is assured. Unfortunately, the best clue to its origin—and perhaps also to the origin of the others—is a faded and illegible chalk inscription on the right side of the upper drawer.

This table has been in Habersham (now Banks) County since it was made and has been owned continuously in one family. According to family history it was made by an ancestor.

1. See Henry D. Green, *Furniture of the Georgia Piedmont before 1830* (Atlanta: High Museum of Art, 1976), pp. 58-59; Jane Webb Smith, *Georgia's Legacy: History Charted Through the Arts* (Athens, Ga.: University of Georgia Press, 1983), pp. 144-45; and Museum of Early Southern Decorative Arts, files S-6418 and S-6419.

51

BLANKET CHEST

Possibly DeKalb County, ca. 1825
Made by unknown artisan
Yellow pine
22 x 45½ x 17¾ inches
Descent in family of original owner
Private collection
Color illustration on page 56

The painted decoration on this blanket chest depicts foliage–possibly the broad native tulip poplar leaf, the water leaf, the bay leaf, and the laurel leaf. This treatment differs from the imitation wood or marble graining seen on other Piedmont furniture and architectural woodwork.

A close examination of the paint layers on this chest reveals the complex technique used to achieve the final effect. First, red paint was applied to the end grain of the corner dovetail joints; the minerals in the paint, ocher and iron oxide, acted as preservatives at these open joints. The entire blanket chest was then given a prime coat of cream-colored paint, over which was applied an ocher paint. Traces of this yellow are visible on the molding of the lid and on the base, indicating that these areas of the chest were originally painted. Next, the decorative leaf patterns were drawn in pencil. A long-haired brush dipped in brown paint was used to color the broad tulip poplar leaves and the skeletal water leaf on the case front. The bay and laurel leaf motifs were painted on the ends of the case, and a design simulating a wood burl was painted on the back of the case. (This burl is similar to one in poplar trees caused by a disease which was eradicated by the 1850s.) Areas not covered with the leaf design were decorated with a leather graining comb. The entire chest then received a finish coat of highly refined varnish.[1]

This distinctive chest descended in the Chesnut family, accompanied by a note written by Margaret Amanda Chesnut Banks (1907-1979) identifying it as an old family piece. Another piece of Georgia furniture that descended in the same family is a chest of drawers, ca. 1830-1850, attributed to Alexander Chesnut (1809-1881).[2] The Chesnut family moved from South Carolina to Georgia in 1804; the 1830 Federal Census records them as residents of DeKalb County.

1. Technical information was provided by period design consultant Reneau de Beauchamp of Decatur, Georgia, during his examination of the blanket chest on February 22, 1990.
2. William W. Griffin et al., *Neat Pieces: The Plain-Style Furniture of 19th Century Georgia* (Atlanta: Atlanta Historical Society, 1983), p. 141.

52

Blanket Chest

Walton County, ca. 1840
Made by unknown artisan
Yellow pine
27 x 42½ x 19¾ inches
Descent in family of early owner
Private collection
Color illustration on page 56

This and a related blanket chest have robust, shaped skirts and, on three sides, original ornamentation in yellow, green, and red paint.[1] On both chests, dotted and linear blocks create a paneled effect, and stippling accents the bold curves of the skirt.

Both of the painted chests have histories in Walton County. This one descended in the Mitchell family of Walnut Grove. The last family member to own it was Kate Elizabeth Mitchell, who inherited it from her father, Charles Edgar Mitchell (1877-1954); he had acquired it from his father, Jett T. Mitchell (1822-1898), an attorney, Civil War captain, and farmer.

This chest has a hidden interior compartment. The right side of the visible compartment, the till, lifts free of the chest to reveal a secret box beneath.

1. The other chest is in the collection of the High Museum of Art, 1985.17.

53

QUILT

Oglethorpe County, 1835
Made by Charlotta Barnett Hardman (1801-1886)
Cotton
94 x 76 inches
Marks: "Lottie Barnett Hardman/1835" in ink
on back
Descent in family of maker
Lent by Mary Sue Jones Barron
Color illustration on page 57

Multi-colored, multi-patterned calico fabrics cut in
small diamonds were used in concentric hexagons to
build this large six-pointed Star of the East quilt. Cut-

ting the fabrics, laying out the pattern, and stitching
the pieces required great skill to ensure that the quilt
top would lie flat.

Various star patterns had become popular
throughout the country by 1830. Some had a large
central star; others formed an overall grid of equal-
sized stars; others, like this one, combined a central
star with smaller stars.

The ink inscription on the back identifies the maker
and date and appears to be in the same handwriting
as that on the quilt made by Charlotta's sister-in-law,
Emaline Bridges Barnett (no. 54). Both quilts have
descended in the family of Mrs. Hardman.

54

QUILT

Commerce, Jackson County, 1840
Made by Emaline Bridges Barnett (ca. 1822-1840)
Cotton
94 x 82½ inches
Marks: "Made by/Emaline Barnett/1840" in ink
on back
Descent in family of maker
Lent by Mary Sue Jones Barron

This Pumpkin Seed or Melon Patch pattern is executed with a thin appliquéd strip of red print calico.
This is an unusual use of this pattern, which is more
often in the quilt stitching itself, either on the appliquéd pieces or on the background. Calico, an inexpensive, small-patterned cotton, came into common
use on quilts in the mid-nineteenth century, replacing
the imported block- and roller-printed chintzes used
earlier in the century.

Emaline Barnett's family knows little about her.
In 1835 she married John D. Barnett in Oglethorpe
County. She died in 1840, the year she made this quilt.
Her sister-in-law, Charlotta Barnett Hardman, also
made a quilt included in this exhibition (no. 53).

Detail

55

COVERLET

Newtown, Madison County, ca. 1840
Attributed to Elizabeth David (1784-1859)
Wool and cotton
94 x 74 inches
Descent in family of maker
Lent by Mrs. Roper Bell David, Sr.
Color illustration on page 59

This coverlet is one of three that descended in the
family of Elizabeth David. This one was woven in two
sections in the Double Bow Knot/Blooming Flower

Variation, a popular pattern of the period. The red
and teal colors were achieved by using natural dyes;
the red derived from the root of the madder plant,
and the teal from a blend of marigold and indigo. The
other coverlets are a rose and black geometric pattern
and a green and black Pine Tree pattern.

Eleven years after Elizabeth David's death, her
husband's estate inventory listed an unusually large
number of bedcoverings, including "17 coverlids," as
well as equipment and supplies for making yarn,
thread, and coverlets. The estate included:

2 bedsteads and beddings	$20.00 each
1 bed pillow and counterpain	10.00
17 coverlids	50.00
1 lot of bed covers	35.00
1 lot counterpain sheet &c	50.00
1 lot counterpain sheet	20.00
running g___ for gin and thrasher	15.00
2 gin bands	5.00
2 gins	5.00
2 spinning wheels	1.00
warping bars	1.00
1 loom	2.00
1 lot of wool	5.00
1 bale of cotton	50.00

Although there is no direct evidence that Elizabeth
David wove coverlets, the David estate inventory
clearly suggests that someone on his property was
spinning and weaving wool and cotton.

Detail

56

SIDEBOARD

Augusta, Richmond County, or Athens,
Clarke County, ca. 1830
Made by unknown artisan
Mahogany and mahogany veneers; yellow pine
56¾ x 60 x 22⅛ inches
Descent in family of original owner
Lent by Augusta H. Warren

Family history traces ownership of this piece back to
Martha Gresham and George Harper Lester of Lex-
ington in Oglethorpe County. It is believed that one of
them owned the sideboard before their marriage in

1843. Both had been residents of Oglethorpe County.

The Lesters' stylish sideboard, with its mahogany
veneers and spiral turned columns, was made by a
skillful cabinetmaker, probably one working in an
urban area like Augusta or Athens. The flame-grained
mahogany veneers on the inset door panels are high-
lighted by cross-cut veneers on the frame. Instead of
using standard drawer pulls on the top tier of drawers, the cabinetmaker fashioned undercut hand pulls
on their lower edges. The lower bottle drawers have
pressed glass pulls.

57

DESK AND BOOKCASE

Yellow Dirt, Heard County, ca. 1840
Made by Joseph Hollingsworth (1797-1859)
or Levi Hollingsworth (1822-1899)
Yellow pine
73½ x 45½ x 23⅝ inches
Descent in family of original owner
Lent by Edward G. and Mary Martin Davis Bowen

This desk and bookcase was made by Joseph Hollingsworth or his son Levi. Originally from Laurens
District, South Carolina, the Hollingsworth family
arrived in Georgia in 1815, settling first in DeKalb
County, then Rockdale County in 1834, and finally,
after 1834, in Heard County. There Joseph Hollingsworth established a sawmill, a gristmill, and a
cotton gin on a creek which fed into the Chattahoochee River. These businesses continued to operate
until they were burned by Federal troops.

The desk was made for George B. Davis (ca. 1796-
1860s), a Virginian who came to Wilkes County as a
child. He lived in Coweta County before moving to
Fayette County in the late 1850s.

This desk is similar to one made in Wilkes County
during the same period.[1] Both were made in two
sections. Their bookcases have flared cornices and a
simple molding above glazed doors. This example
adds a tier of half-width drawers beneath the doors
and a full-width drawer in the table section. Both
have straight tapering legs mortised to the table
section. Another similar piece is the desk and bookcase made by Alexander G. Slappey in Fort Valley
(see no. 21).

1. William W. Griffin et al., *Neat Pieces: The Plain-Style
   Furniture of 19th Century Georgia* (Atlanta: Atlanta
   Historical Society, 1983), p. 155.

58

CHEST OF DRAWERS

Crabapple, Fulton County, ca. 1840
Made by Azariah Denny Gentry (ca. 1811–ca. 1890)
Walnut; yellow pine
48¾ x 73 x 24 inches
Descent in family of maker
Lent by Mary Rucker Stewart

The three tiers of drawers are the most distinctive features of this broad chest, the only one of this design seen during the survey. The vertical medial posts on the side panels and the French-style corner brackets at the four front feet are also notable. The drawer pulls are not original.

According to family tradition, the cabinetmaker was Denny Gentry, who was born in the Anderson District of South Carolina. Between 1830 and 1840, he settled in the Crabapple community of Milton (now Fulton) County. Military records show that he was serving in the Cherokee Legion of the Confederate Army between July 1863 and January 1864. He returned to Crabapple, where he was still living in the late 1880s.

59

BOOKCASE

Probably Athens, Clarke County, after 1844
Made by unknown artisan
Yellow pine
87 x 57 x 10½ inches
Descent in family of first owner
Lent by Mrs. Hugh Smiley Stanley

This freestanding bookcase is one of a group of four Gothic-style bookcases that have descended in three different Athens families. All four of the bookcases have their original faux mahogany grained finishes. The square end pillars all have crenelated tops, and the pillars on three also have quatrefoils and arches.

This bookcase descended in the family of Julia Tabitha Ann Pope Stanley (1824-1894). A second bookcase descended in the family of Mr. and Mrs. Charles Alexander Scudder of Athens. Two others were in the family of Governor Wilson Lumpkin. Lumpkin's descendants always assumed his bookcases had been made in Milledgeville while he was serving as Governor, because the state capitol building in Milledgeville was also in the Gothic style. But Governor Lumpkin lived in Athens after leaving office, and the appearance of two similar bookcases in the Athens area makes it likely that all were made there.

60

BOWL AND SALVER

Augusta, Richmond County, ca. 1840-1860
Made by Joseph Steadman Clark
Clark, Rackett & Co.; Clark & Co.
Silver
Bowl: 6½ x 6 inches, salver: ¾ x 8 inches
Marks: "Mary S. Clark/from her/Father" engraved
on each piece; "Clark, Rackett & Co" in rectangle
stamped on inside of lid; "Clark & Co" in rectangle
stamped on bottom of bowl and salver
Private collection

This is the only known covered bowl and salver
among Georgia silver forms. The maker's marks and
inscriptions show that the pieces were made by Joseph
Steadman Clark's firm and given by him to his daughter Mary (born in 1840), the first of four children
born to Caroline E. Mealing and Joseph Clark.[1]

Francis Clark of Connecticut established himself as
a silversmith in Augusta in 1816. He may have been
a partner in the firm Clark, Rackett & Company
(1840-1852) with Horace and Joseph Steadman Clark
and George Rackett.[2] After Rackett's death in 1852,
Horace and Joseph renamed the business Clark &
Co. When Horace died in 1854, Joseph continued to
operate the business as Clark & Co. until the early
1860s.[3] In the 1860 Census, he is listed as a "dealer
of fancy goods," whereas in 1850 he had been listed
simply as a "jeweler."

1. Two different company marks appear on these pieces—
   Clark, Rackett & Co. (1840-1852) and Clark & Co.
   (1852-ca. 1860). This may indicate that the pieces were
   all made in 1852, the date common to both marks, or at
   different times.
2. George Barton Cutten, *The Silversmiths of Georgia*
   (Savannah, Ga.: Pigeonhole Press, 1958), pp. 24-25.
3. A tea service marked "Clark & Co." has recently been
   added to the collection of the High Museum of Art,
   1987.174.1-.3.

61

MASONIC APRON

LaGrange, Troup County, 1842
Made by Nancy Coleman Ferrell (1799-1889)
Satin and linen
17 x 15⅝ inches
Descent in family of maker and original owner
Troup County Historical Society–Archives

In 1842 the Union Masonic Lodge of Free and
Accepted Masons in LaGrange was chartered. This
apron of the lodge's Grand Master, Judge Blount
Coleman Ferrell, was made by his mother-in-law,
Nancy Coleman Ferrell.[1]

The apron is the badge of a Mason, worn for
lodge meetings, processions, funerals, and other cere-
monies. The symbols represent the stages of a Mason's
voyage through life and indicate rank. This apron
incorporates many Masonic symbols: the sun, radiating light to guide the Mason's search for intellectual
truth; globes, expressive of the universality of Freemasonry; the beehive symbolizing industry; the
all-seeing eye of God; geometric symbols related to
stonemasonry; and the pillars of Solomon's temple,
the home of eternal life.[2] This is the most ornate of the
four Masonic aprons documented in the survey.

1. Nancy Coleman was the second wife of Mickleberry
   Ferrell. Their daughter Sarah married her double first
   cousin, Judge Blount Coleman Ferrell.
2. Letter from Steven Myhre, Worshipful Master, Solomon's
   Lodge No. 1, Savannah, to Pamela Wagner, March 12,
   1990.

62

HIGHCHAIR

Hephzibah, Richmond County, 1844
Attributed to John Franklin Carswell (1817-1882)
Hickory and birch, with oak splint seat
33½ x 12⅜ x 12 inches
Descent in family of maker
Private collection

According to Carswell family history, this chair was made by John Franklin Carswell, a graduate of Mercer Institute who owned a grocery at 124 Broad Street in Augusta. In 1843 he married Mary P. Kilpatrick of Augusta. He made this chair in 1844, shortly after the birth of their first child, James Alexander. By 1850 Carswell and his growing family had moved to Burke County, where he owned a farm.

With its bowed arched slats and turned posts, this highchair is similar to others found in Georgia. The oak splint seat replaced the original hide one.

63

CORNER CUPBOARD

Red Oak, Fulton County, ca. 1850
Made by James Ellis Lee (1822-1902)
Tulip poplar
80 x 52¾ inches
Descent in family of maker
Lent by James E. Lee, D.V.M.

The distinctive feature of this corner cupboard is the original painted graining, a brown and amber simulation of oak. Few early Georgia pieces have retained their original painted finishes. Other elements—the deep composite top molding and the low simple bracket feet—are typical of mid-nineteenth-century Georgia corner cupboards. Like other Georgia examples, this cupboard was built as a single tall unit, with horizontal molding extending to the side edges, framing the sides and front. On the interior, there are two fixed shelves in the upper section and one in the lower.

According to family history, this corner cupboard was made by James Ellis Lee, in whose family it has descended. Born in South Carolina, Lee moved to Red Oak in 1830. In 1845, he married Elizabeth A. Baker, and they settled in the Red Oak area.

64

QUILT

Barnesville, Upson County, 1849
Made by R. Elizabeth Belah Riviere (1826-1888)
Cotton
94 x 84 inches
Marks: "R.E. Belah/Upson Cty Ga 1849" and
"WHEN THIS YOU/SEE REMEMBER/
LIZZIE/1849" stitched in corners
Descent in family of maker
Lent by Mrs. Morrill T. Hutchinson

Fine stitching joins the diamond-shaped calico pieces
to create this six-pointed variation of the eight-point
Sunburst pattern. Nine full stars and seven half stars,
all of equal size, are arranged in rows, and diamond
shapes in the border echo the shape of the calico
pieces. The maker's name, date, and an inscription are
discreetly stitched in two corners.

Family descendants believe that Lizzie Belah completed this quilt just before her marriage in 1849 to
Francis Riviere.

65

QUILT

Oak Grove Plantation, Union Point,
Greene County, after 1840
Made by Anne Barnett Hart (1786-1863)
Cotton
110 x 110 inches
Descent in family of maker
Private collection

According to family tradition, Anne Barnett Hart
made this bedcover around 1804, prior to her 1810
marriage to Thomas Hart. However, the pieced and
appliquéd star pattern and the roller-printed fabrics
suggest a date after 1840. Perhaps she made the
quilt for her daughter Georgianna America Hart

(1832-1907) at the time of her marriage to James
William Horton in 1852. The quilt has descended
from Georgianna.

By the 1840s, the eight-pointed Star of Bethlehem
quilt pattern was popular throughout America. The
motif had many regional names: in the midwest, it
was Prairie Star; in Massachusetts, it was often Ship's
Wheel; and in Texas, Lone Star.

Anne Barnett Hart selected a variety of blue,
brown, and green roller-printed chintz fabrics for
the tiny diamond pieces which form her stars. She
followed a common practice of using contrasting fabric for her border, selecting an aqua and rose floral
pattern.

66

WARDROBE

Probably Athens, Clarke County, ca. 1850-1875
Made by unknown artisan
Tulip poplar and yellow pine; yellow pine
88 x 78 x 30 inches
Label: "G T Murrell/Winterville/Ga"
Descent in family of early owner
Lent by Mr. and Mrs. James D. Carter

The most distinctive feature of this wardrobe is the unusually deep overhanging cavetto cornice, echoed in the exaggerated arches of the door panels. The original faux mahogany graining was badly worn when the wardrobe was sold at the 1979 estate sale of the last Murrell owner; what remained of the graining was removed by the current owners. (Mahogany graining appears on a group of bookcases from Athens; see no. 59). On the interior, there are four shelves to the left of the center stile, and a rod with seven hooks to the right.

Nailed to the back of the wardrobe is a cardboard label, possibly a shipping label, which associates the piece with George T. Murrell (1848-ca. 1900-10), an early owner. In 1875 Murrell and his wife, Leila Wade Morton, inherited from her father three tracts of land in Winterville in Clarke County. By 1878 they had built a large home there. The railroad from Athens to Union Point established a stop in front of their home, which came to be known as Murrell Station.

67

QUILT

Greenville, Meriwether County, ca. 1860
Made by Mary Jane Dixon Render (1832-1902)
Cotton
90 x 88½ inches
Descent in family of maker
Lent by Mary Jane Hill Crayton

A variety of nature motifs are combined on this quilt:
holly leaves and wreaths in the appliquéd pattern, and
pineapples and acorns in the background stitching.
The undulating vine provides a border for the nine
individual blocks and for the whole quilt.

Mary Jane Dixon Render lived on a cotton plantation just south of Greenville. Her descendants also
own two other quilts that she made: a six-pointed
variation of the eight-point Sunburst (see no. 64) and
one in the Broken Star pattern. The background
stitching on both is the running diamond pattern.

68

BEDSTEAD

Marietta, Cobb County, after 1850
Made by Dix Fletcher (1803-1886)
Yellow pine
60¾ x 57 x 82 inches
Descent in family of maker
Lent by Mr. and Mrs. Bayard McIntosh Cole

This is one of two bedsteads made by Dix Fletcher.
Its tall paneled headboard has an elaborate cresting:
a scroll-end board capped by a turned crest rail with
acorn terminals. Acorns also cap the tapered head
and foot posts.

Dix Fletcher moved to Savannah in 1837 from

Phillipston, Massachusetts. According to family history, he worked as a cabinetmaker and a cotton factor
in Savannah, until his warehouse burned in 1849. The
1849 Directory of the City of Savannah identifies him
as a carpenter residing at 43 Liberty Street and working at 31 Habersham Street. In 1850 Fletcher and his
family moved to Marietta, where the Census lists him
as a landlord. By 1860 he was operating the Fletcher
House, one of Marietta's resort hotels. Descendants
own the hotel's ledger and a sheet of hotel letterhead
stationery which reads: "Fletcher House at railroad
depot, Dix Fletcher, proprietor; Marietta, Georgia."

69

CHEST OF DRAWERS WITH MIRROR

Cobb County, ca. 1860
Made by Green Berry Bentley (1832-1905)
Walnut; tulip poplar; mirror
73 x 40¾ x 18¾ inches
Descent in family of maker
Lent by Mr. and Mrs. Fred D. Bentley, Sr.

In keeping with the fashion of the mid-century,
Green Berry Bentley applied many carved details to
his bureau, among them a filigree scroll at the crest of
the oval mirror, the beading on the mirror frame, split
spindles on the case, inset paneled drawer fronts, and
scrolling brackets supporting the mirror and adjacent

to the feet. These ornamental motifs are related to
Elizabethan and Rococo Revival designs popular
before the Civil War.

This chest of drawers descended in the family of
the cabinetmaker. Originally from South Carolina,
Green Berry Bentley moved to the Gritter District of
Cobb County during the 1850s. Census records from
1860 to 1900 list him as a farmer.

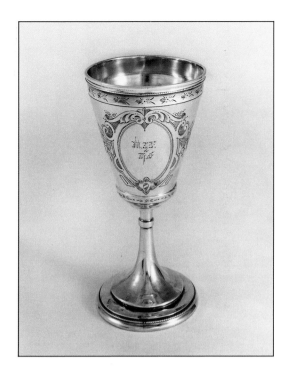

70

PENDANT

Possibly Columbus, Muscogee County, 1856
Made by unknown artisan
Gold and diamond
2⅞ x 2⅝ inches
Marks: "FRATERNAL OFFERING FROM
DARLEY CHAPTER NO 7, COLUMBUS, GA.,/
TO M.E.H.P. PHILLIP T. SCHLEY." and "MAY
1st,/1856." engraved on one side; "HOLINESS TO
THE LORD." and the names of the sons of Jacob
engraved on other side
Descent in family of original owner
Lent by Dr. and Mrs. Philip T. Schley

In addition to the inscription to Phillip Schley, this
small pendant is engraved with religious and Masonic
symbols. On one side are drawn the following
images: a book, presumably the Bible, open to Chap-
ters VI, VII, and VIII, and a covered urn centering a
miter inset with a radiating sun; below are the names
of the sons of Jacob ("Judah, Issachar, Zebulon,
Reuben, Simeon, Gad, Ephraim, Manassah,
Benjamin, Dan, Asher, Naphtali") who were the
leaders of the twelve tribes of Israel, and their location around the Tabernacle as described in the Old
Testament Book of Numbers. On the other side are
a triangle and several pseudo-Hebrew characters.

Phillip T. Schley was born in 1800 in Louisville,
Georgia. An attorney, he apparently moved to
Columbus by 1836. In that year he was a founding
member and prominent leader of the Darley Chapter
of the Masons. In 1849 he laid the cornerstone of
Temperance Hall, the Masons' new meeting center.
The 1850 Census records him living in Columbus
with his wife and six children; by 1860 he and his
youngest son had moved to Savannah where his older
brothers were living.

Gold pieces of Georgia origin are extremely rare.
This and another made for Roswell King are the only
two gold pendants recorded in the survey. Neither
has a maker's mark, so it cannot be determined if the
pieces were made in Georgia or if they were made out
of Georgia gold, which was mined near Dahlonega
between 1829 and 1861.

71

GOBLET

Macon, Bibb County, ca. 1860
Probably engraved by Lewis H. Wing (1837-?)
Made by Albert Coles and Company, New York City
(working 1836-1876)
Silver
6½ x 3¼ inches
Marks: "M.V.F./to/H.F" engraved on side within
cartouche; "A/C," eagle, and head stamped on
bottom; "L.H. WING/COIN/MACON/GA."
incised on bottom
Descent in family of original owner
Lent by Margaret Hatcher Wagner

This is one of a set of thirty-six goblets. The engraved
inscription, "M.V.F. to H.F" indicates that they were
a gift from Mary Virginia Crocker Felton (1835-1916)
to William Hamilton Felton (1828-1906). The
Feltons, residents of Marshallville in Macon County,
were married in 1850.

Lewis Wing was listed in the 1860 Federal Census
for Bibb County as a jeweler from Vermont. Two
previous Georgia exhibitions have included silver
pieces made by Coles and retailed by Wing; all three
have similar engraved cartouches surrounding the
inscriptions.[1]

1. Callie Huger Efird and Katharine Gross Farnham,
   Georgia Collects American Silver, 1780-1870 (Atlanta:
   High Museum of Art, 1970), no. 292; Jane Webb Smith,
   Georgia's Legacy: History Charted Through the Arts
   (Athens, Ga.: University of Georgia Press, 1983),
   no. 139.

72

JEWELRY BOX

Augusta, Richmond County, ca. 1860-1881
Made by Charles A. Ladeveze (1830-1881)
White pine, silk, and mirror
4½ x 11⅝ x 8½ inches
Label: "CHARLES A. LADEVEZE/Successor to R.A.
HARPER,/PICTURE-FRAME/MANUFACTORY,/
32 McIntosh-Street,/AUGUSTA, GA." on bottom
Private collection
Color illustration on page 59

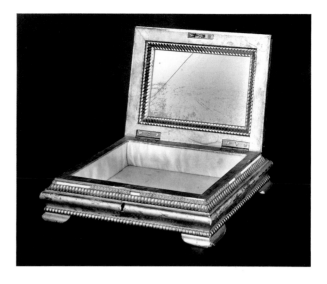

This rare box is the only labeled piece by a free person of color that was documented in the survey.[1] It is made of gessoed and gilt picture frame moldings, and has a paper label glued to the bottom.

Ladeveze was a mulatto whose French-born father, Raymond Ladeveze, lived in Haiti before moving to Augusta in the 1820s. The 1860 Census lists Charles Ladeveze as a cabinetmaker, residing next to his sister, Laura Harper, who was married to Robert Harper, a piano tuner (perhaps the R. A. Harper named on

Ladeveze's label). The manufacturing census for 1880 records that Ladeveze was a "picture framer," employing four people in his shop. Charles's oldest son, John, appears that year in the Federal Census as a "cabinetmaker." Another of his sons, Charles R., trained with his father and then opened his own picture frame shop in Savannah.

Charles Ladeveze's estate inventory includes picture frame molding, frames, easels, framed pictures and mirrors, a miter box, vice, and grindstone.

1. Edward J. Cashin, *The Story of Augusta* (Augusta, Ga.: Richmond County Board of Education, 1980), p. 184.

73

CRADLE

Columbus, Muscogee County, or Atlanta, Fulton County, ca. 1864
Made by Gottlieb Nelson Aenchbacher (1839-1903)
Walnut; yellow pine
24½ x 38 x 38 inches
Descent in family of maker
Lent by Byron Attridge

Samuel Aenchbacher, a tailor, emigrated with his family from Bern, Switzerland, and settled in Columbus before 1850, the year they first appear on the Federal Census. Nelson, one of several sons, moved to Atlanta; the 1880 Census lists Martha and Nelson

Aenchbacher living at 90 Jones Avenue, Atlanta, along with their sixteen-year-old son, John L., in whose family the cradle has descended. According to family tradition, the cradle was made for John.

74

BEDSTEAD

Thomson, McDuffie County, ca. 1865
Made by William Sheppard Smith (1825-1889)
Yellow pine
76½ x 57¾ x 79¼ inches
Descent in family of maker
Lent by Kellie Bush Dobbins

Scrolled head- and footboards, which were popular in Georgia in the mid-nineteenth century,[1] are here tenoned into octagonal posts which have pointed finials. The footboard has a rolled crest rail with ball and spool turnings. The side rails are fitted for rope supports. The pine bedstead was originally painted.[2]

William Sheppard Smith, a farmer, owned Smith's

Mill on Maddox Creek. He used his skills as a woodworker in constructing his mill, a two-story home, and all of its furnishings around 1865. During the Civil War, he had worked as a wheelwright repairing cannons for the Confederate supply shop in Augusta. This bed is the only piece made by Smith that has descended in this branch of his family.

1. William W. Griffin et al., *Neat Pieces: The Plain-Style Furniture of 19th Century Georgia* (Atlanta: Atlanta Historical Society, 1983), pp. 66-67.
2. The present owner reports that at least five layers of paint were stripped from the bed. No traces of the original paint remain.

75

Quilt

Sunnyside, Spalding County, ca. 1870
Made by Mary Elizabeth Manley Malaier
(1849-1931)
Cotton
94 x 92 inches
Mark: "M. E. Manley" in later stitching
Descent in family of maker
Lent by Ava Malaier Hill
Color illustration on page 59

The most unusual feature of this appliquéd quilt is the ruching of the flower petals. Ruching is a technique of pleating or ruffling fabric to set it in high relief against a flat background. Also noteworthy is the

quilt stitching; the tightly spaced stitches form garlands and oak leaves, two uncommon patterns, on the white background. The brilliant reds and greens were produced by aniline dyes, introduced after 1865.

This quilt descended in the Malaier family, in which the design is known as the Dahlia pattern. According to the owner, the name "M. E. Manley" was added to the quilt at a later date, to record the maker's identity.

76

VASE

Stevens Pottery, Baldwin County, ca. 1876-1900
Made by Stevens Brothers & Company
(working 1876-ca. 1900)
Stoneware with manganese-colored glaze
10 x 10¾ inches
Marks: "STEVENS BROS &- CO" impressed
on base
Lent by Mr. and Mrs. William A. Fickling, Jr.
Color illustration on page 61

This is one of three pieces of Stevens Brothers & Company pottery found during the survey, and is the only example of manganese or Rockingham glaze. Most Georgia-made pottery was turned and then finished with alkaline or Albany slip glazes. The molded classical form, with its lobed bowl and foliate rim, is also unusual.

The pottery's founder, Henry Stevens (1813-1876), emigrated from England in 1831, which would account for the stylish glaze and form of this vase. Stevens established a sawmill and lumber business in 1854 south of Milledgeville. In 1858 discovering high quality clays on his land, he founded Stevens Pottery

there. Upon his death in 1876, his sons continued the business, changing the name to Stevens Brothers & Company. In addition to this decorative vase, the firm made utilitarian objects such as jugs, flower pots, jars, sewer pipes, bricks, and chimney tops.

77

ROCKING CHAIR

Marietta, Cobb County, ca. 1875-1880
Made by Brumby Chair Company
(working 1875-1944, 1972-1989)
Red oak with cane seat
47 x 28 x 35 inches
High Museum of Art, gift of the Rocker Shop
of Marietta

The Brumby Chair Company made rockers in sizes ranging from "jumbo" to smaller lady's versions and children's chairs. When these chairs were first manufactured, the shape and decoration of the head rests and turnings on the posts and stretchers reflected the Arts and Crafts style and Colonial Revival styles. The latter is seen in this chair, one of the earliest of the Brumby models.

The company was founded in 1875 by two brothers, Thomas M. and James Brumby. In the 1879-1880 manufacturing census, the Brumby Furniture Chair Factory reported the annual value of their product at $30,000. At its height, before World War II, the company was one of the largest manufacturing firms in the state, employing about 400 workers. Difficulty in hiring workers and obtaining high quality woods led to the closing of the company in 1944 and again in 1989.

78

QUILT

Atlanta, Fulton County, ca. 1880-1900
Made by Margaret Josephine VanDyke Inman
(1849-1920)
Velvet, silk, and satin
55 x 56 inches
Descent in family of maker
Lent by William Edward Rudolph
Color illustration on page 61

Elaborate crazy quilts were primarily decorative
rather than utilitarian. Unlike the cotton pieced and
appliquéd quilts of earlier decades, crazy quilts were
usually made of relatively expensive fabrics such as
velvet, silk, and satin.

Mrs. Inman organized the irregularly shaped
patches of her quilt by using a diagonal black velvet
grid. She pieced and decorated the individual patches
with a variety of delicate stitches and embroidered
motifs including flowers, fans, birds, and other ani-

mals. Also worked in embroidery are the initials of
her five children: Annie Martin, Josephine VanDyke,
Hugh Theodore, Edward Hamilton, and Louise. The
lace border is an unusual feature of this quilt.

Margaret VanDyke Inman was the daughter of
Eliza Ann Deaderick and Thomas Nixon VanDyke.
Raised in Athens, Tennessee, she attended the Athens
Female College there, and later enrolled at DePauw
College in Indiana. In 1871 she married Hugh
Theodore Inman. They lived in New York City until
1874, when they built their first house in Atlanta, at
the corner of Peachtree and Harris Streets. By 1892
Inman, a banker, was one of Georgia's nine million-
aires.[1] In 1909 they built a new home on West
Peachtree, near 5th Street.

1. Sidney Ratner, ed., *New Light on the History of Great
   American Fortunes: American Millionaires of 1892 and
   1902* (New York: Augustus M. Kelley, 1953), p. 11.

79

BEDSPREAD

Atlanta, Fulton County, ca. 1880
Made by Kate Harman Orme (1850-1917)
Linen and cotton
89 x 93 inches
Descent in family of maker
Lent by Callie Huger Efird

This bedspread is one of a small group of late nine-teenth-century white-on-white needlework bedcovers documented by the Georgia Decorative Arts Survey. This is the only one with an elaborate embroidered center panel.

A heavy white cotton thread was used to embroider the designs onto a linen background. The large cen-tral panel is skillfully worked with an overall pattern of flowers and scrolling tendrils around a central medallion. Floral crocheted lace bands join the sec-tions of the spread, and a scrolled crocheted lace band forms the outer border.

Kate Harman Orme's descendants own many examples of her crocheted and embroidered work, including a large crocheted bedspread in a Sun pat-tern. An embroidered bedspread by her mother, Absyllah Holmes Callaway Harman, is also in this exhibition (no. 80).

80

BEDSPREAD

Atlanta, Fulton County, ca. 1880
Made by Absyllah Holmes Callaway Harman
(1821-1918)
Cotton
92 x 86 inches
Descent in family of maker
Lent by Callie Huger Efird

This heavy bedspread is made up of small knitted squares which were worked separately and then crocheted together; a wider crocheted border was applied to the sides of the spread. Three different stitches were used to make the knitted squares: the reverse stockinette, bobble (or "popcorn"), and palm frond. The overall diamond pattern was popular on American handwork of the mid to late nineteenth century. Knitting, quilting, and other needlework patterns and instructions were popularized nationally in such magazines as the widely read *Godey's Lady's Book and Magazine*, published from 1838 to 1890.

Also documented in the survey were two other bedcovers made by Mrs. Harman: a crocheted panel bedspread and a Double Irish Chain quilt.

Detail

81

CRADLE

Maysville, Banks County, ca. 1890
Made by William Alvin O'Kelley (1831-1905)
Hickory, maple, and pine
38 x 20 x 39 inches
Descent in family of maker
High Museum of Art, gift of Mattie Lou O'Kelley

This cradle was made by William Alvin O'Kelley for his grandson, William Augustus O'Kelley (1890-1985). The maker was a farmer and wagonmaker who lived first in Gordon County, then in Banks County. The equipment and skills he used to make wagon wheels—steaming and bending wood in a caul—were useful in shaping the headboard and footboard of this cradle.

Of the twelve cradles documented in the survey, this and two others are very similar, having thin bent

and scribed posts reminiscent of nineteenth-century Windsor chairs. One of the others has a long history of ownership in Fort Valley, Peach County; the history of the third is unknown.

82

DROP-FRONT DESK

Augusta, Richmond County, 1878
Made by Caspar Hermann Johannsen (1828-1895)
Yellow pine
71 x 45½ x 21½ inches
Marks: "C. H. Johannsen Augusta/the maker of this
piece furniture/(of Georgia pine)/October [illegible]
1878" in pencil on dustboard under second drawer,
and a similar inscription
Descent in family of original owner
Private collection

This unusually sophisticated and complex desk has
a drop-front writing surface which slides under the
interior desk section, and a mechanism in the inner
cupboard which releases the lock on the full-width
drawers.

This is the only known piece by C. H. Johannsen.
The 1880 Census records him as a German-born
grocer, and indicates that he was in Georgia by 1867,
when his son was born.

The desk was made for Daniel DeBruce Hack
(1816-1881), whose father came from Massachusetts
and founded the Richmond Factory, a cotton and
wool textile manufacturing mill on Spirit Creek,
south of Augusta.[1] By 1880 Daniel Hack owned the
factory, operated a flour mill, and was an investor in
the new Augusta Savings Bank. By the time of his
death, he had become a prominent land owner in east
central Georgia.

1. His partners were William, George, and Phillip T. Schley.
   Phillip Schley's pendant is in the exhibition (no. 70).

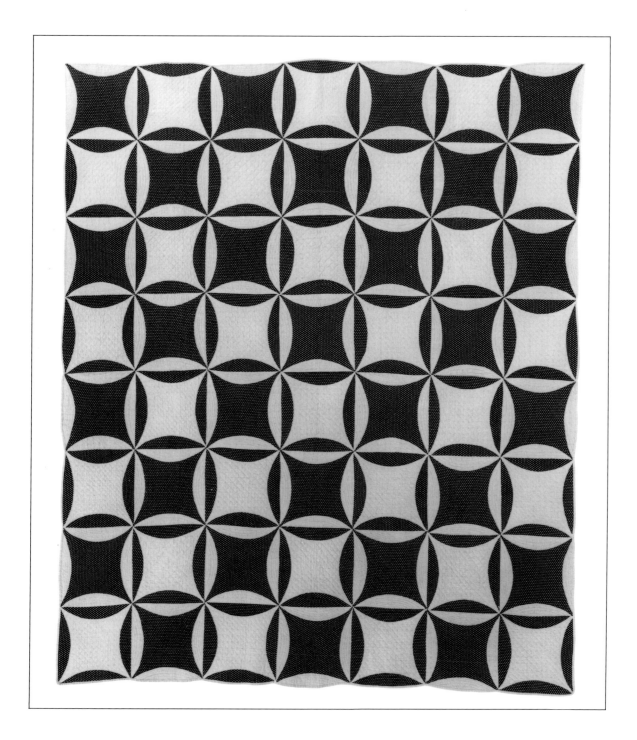

83

QUILT

Woodville, Greene County, 1887
Made by Emmy Durham Guill [Gwill] (1869-1948)
Cotton
88 x 78 inches
Mark: "Emmy Durham/18[8]7" in ink on back
Descent in family of maker
Lent by Carolyn S. McMillan

Emmy Durham married Bluford Alexander Guill in 1896. Although the decade date on the ink inscription on the quilt is illegible, the maker uses her maiden name, which suggests that she made it in 1887, prior to her marriage.

The pattern, here worked out in bold blue and yellow fabrics, is a variation of "Robbing Peter to Pay Paul." Several other Georgia quilts in this pattern were documented by the survey.

84

SIDEBOARD

Lincolnton, Lincoln County, ca. 1894-1910
Made by Harold Charles "Chick" Harris
(1875-ca. 1910)
Yellow pine and mirror
87 x 46¾ x 21¾ inches
Descent in family of maker
Lent by Isabelle C. Pitts
Color illustration on page 60

Like several other pieces documented by the survey, this narrow sideboard is noteworthy for its use of native curly pine. This piece is unusually decorative for Piedmont furniture. Details such as the columns

and the scrolling on the crest indicate the maker's familiarity with factory-made furniture.

This sideboard is one of a few pieces known today which Chick Harris made for local residents and institutions. Two of the other pieces, a desk and a pulpit, also use local curly yellow pine.

Harris was born in northern Alabama, where his parents had settled after living in South Carolina and Georgia. By 1894 Harris had moved to Georgia, where he married Lula Burn of Columbia County. The 1900 Census listed Harris as "a mechanic," and placed his family in Lincoln County.

85

QUILT

Dallas, Paulding County, 1897
Made by Narcissa Caroline Woodall Pearson
(1849-1911), Ada Mae Pearson (1878-1961), and
Georgia Ellen Pearson (1880-1959)
Cotton
71¼ x 85¼ inches
Marks: "1897" and embroidered names and initials
Descent in family of maker
Private collection
Color illustration on page 61

This visually complex quilt combines elements of earlier pieced quilts and late-century crazy quilts. Like
the pieced quilts, the design is built upon the rhythmic
repetition of intricate geometric shapes; like the crazy
quilts, it is enhanced with embroidered inscriptions
and pictures.

Narcissa Caroline Woodall Pearson and her daughters Ada Mae and Georgia Ellen used embroidery to
personalize the quilt, stitching in references to Mrs.
Pearson's other children: "L.T. Pearson" (Lewis Tyler),
"J.L.P." (Judson Lafayette Pearson) and "CCP"

(Clarence Chester Pearson), whose initials are sewn
onto an outline of a child's hand. The baby may be a
reference to Narcissa's two deceased children, Mary
Anne and Lewis Warner. According to family history,
among the men portrayed are George Washington,
Doc Holliday, and Wyatt Earp (the latter two reportedly had traveled through Georgia around this time).

Other embroidered details include short phrases
such as "Remember Me" and "All Love is Sweet,
Given or Returned," nature motifs like flowers and
butterflies, and the date 1897.

This quilt is a variation of the Nine X pattern,
joined by patched round motifs.[1] The plaid fabric is
Alamance, a loosely woven cotton made in the South.
This quilt is one of three attributed to Narcissa Caroline Woodall Pearson. The others, in the Snake and
Bumblebee patterns, used the same solid color fabrics—chrome yellow, dark green, and reddish brown.

1. Barbara Brackman *An Encyclopedia of Pieced Quilt Patterns* (Lawrence, Kans.: Prairie Flower Publishing, 1984),
vol. 6, pp. 394-95.

86

CORNER CUPBOARD

Madison, Morgan County, ca. 1900
Made by The Variety Works, Inc.
Yellow pine
95 3/8 x 65 3/8 inches
Descent in family of company owner
Lent by Dr. Josephine H. Brandon

Corner cupboards were made in Georgia throughout the nineteenth century. This late example follows the standard form: the tall cupboard was made as a single unit, with a simple cornice, paneled doors, and a shaped skirt on which the piece stands. Certain ornamental details, however, are distinctive: the paneled division of the sides, the beading around the panels, and the applied split spindles and bosses.

The cupboard was made by The Variety Works, Inc., in Madison, a firm which manufactured window and door frames, mantels, brackets, newels, rails, balusters, flooring, and ceilings. Reportedly, several of Madison's late nineteenth- and early twentieth-century homes incorporate these locally-made elements.

87

WORK TABLE

Milledgeville, Baldwin County, ca. 1895
Attributed to prisoners at Central State Penitentiary
Possibly chinaberry; tulip poplar
32¼ x 18 x 17¾ inches
Descent in family of original owner
Lent by Mr. and Mrs. A. Alling Jones

As early as 1817, prisoners at the state penitentiary made furniture for state facilities and for sale to the public. According to family history, this work table is part of a suite of bedroom furniture made by prisoners for George W. Hollingshead, Sr., (1886-1955) of Milledgeville, when he was a young boy.

For the period 1817 to 1869, the Central Registry of Prisoners identified the workshops in which each convict worked. During that period, twenty-three were listed as cabinetmakers, chairmakers (including one "windsor chairmaker"), shop joiners, or turners. After 1870 the Registry no longer listed workshop assignments or specific skills, but convicts continued to make furniture until at least 1916.[1]

1. William W. Griffin et al., *Neat Pieces: The Plain-Style Furniture of 19th Century Georgia* (Atlanta: Atlanta Historical Society, 1983), pp. 8, 177-204.

88

TABLE

Macon, Bibb County, ca. 1900
Made by Friedrich Wilhelm Muecke [Mücke]
(1857-1953)
Possibly red cypress
30⅝ x 43½ x 33½ inches
Descent in family of original owner
Lent by Mrs. John Lawrence Brown

The bold curves and the projecting ankles of this table relate it to European furniture designs. The cabinetmaker, F. W. Muecke, came from Austria in 1876 to build an organ at the Philadelphia Centennial Exposition. He returned to Austria for several years before settling in Tennessee in 1880. In 1896 he moved to Macon, where he was employed by the Dohn Furniture Company. The 1910 Professional and Business Directory lists Muecke and Sons Furniture Manufacturers at 614 New Street, where all six of his sons eventually were apprenticed in the cabinetmaking and upholstery business.

The table was made for Robert Hazlehurst Plant (1847-1904), a prominent banker and civic leader in Macon and a director of the Macon and Florida Railroad. According to Plant family history, the table was made of wood from the Red Cypress Lumber Company, which operated in Dougherty County from 1897 to 1910; the wood was shipped to Macon by railroad.

Paperweight

Tallapoosa, Haralson County, ca. 1900-1906
Attributed to Dixie Glass Works
Glass
2³/₄ x 3³/₈ inches
Descent in family of glass company employee
Lent by Mr. and Mrs. William W. Griffin

From the three glassworks operating in Tallapoosa around 1900, the Decorative Arts Survey found only this brilliant blue glass paperweight. It descended in the family of Fred Bosson of the Dixie Glass Works. Bosson, a Swiss emigré, came to the United States at the age of twenty-nine. The 1900 Federal Census records him as a "glassblower" living in Tallapoosa. Also dating from that year is the earliest known record of the Dixie Glass Works, a land deed. Apparently a fire destroyed the factory in 1906.

Three glass houses—the Dixie Glass Works, the Tallapoosa Glass Works, and the Piedmont Glass Works—were among scores of manufacturing, mining, and utilities companies lured to Tallapoosa between 1886 and 1908 by the promotional efforts of the Georgia-Alabama Investment and Development Company. This very successful group of land speculators advertised heavily in northern and midwestern newspapers, promoting Tallapoosa as "a good place for good Yankees." They promised "real estate prices cheaper than in places with one-third the population; to those desiring to establish manufacturing industries, free sites and exemption from taxes for ten years are given."[1] A 1907 state law restricting corporations brought an end to the remarkable Tallapoosa boom.[2]

1. *100 Opinions of the American Press on Tallapoosa, Ga. and the Industrial Enterprise of the Georgia-Alabama Investment and Development Co.* (Boston: L. Barta & Co., 1891), p. 24.
2. Lee S. Trimble, "Historical Sketch of Tallapoosa, Georgia, 1886-1910," typewritten paper. See also Lona Lasseter et al., *Haralson County History Book* (Dallas, Ga.: Taylor Publishing Company, 1983), pp. 21, 23-24.

90

Bedspread

Macon, Bibb County, ca. 1900
Made by Anne Lewis Rushin Willingham (1866-1941)
Cotton
90 x 82 inches
Marks: "BEW" crocheted in center
Descent in family of maker
Lent by Mr. and Mrs. Broadus Estes Willingham IV

The pattern of large diamonds inset with small flowers was worked with fine cotton yarn, which shows off the delicacy of the crocheted filet lace stitching between the flowers. A smaller version of the pattern forms the border. The same pattern was crocheted on a bedspread by Sarah Tucker at about the same time (see no. 40).

In 1885 Anne Lewis Rushin of Tallassee, Alabama, married Broadus Estes Willingham III (1862-1937), who founded Willingham Cotton Mills in Macon. Crocheted on the center of the bedspread are his initials. Their grandson remembers Anne frequently knitting and crocheting, but only this piece and a knitted afghan survive.

Detail

91

COMPOTE

Washington, Wilkes County, ca. 1900
Painted by Mary Martia Sims Latimer (1881-1974)
European porcelain
6 x 9¾ inches
Descent in family of maker
Lent by Mary Latimer Blue

This European porcelain compote is one of a group
of pieces painted by Mary Latimer while she was
studying at St. Joseph's Academy in Washington. Her
descendants believe that she painted the compote and
other pieces (a cup and saucer, platter, plate, and
bowl) prior to her marriage in 1903 to William
Robert Latimer.

Decorating the bowl of the compote is a cluster of
cherries. The exterior is painted with gold leaves on
an aqua ground; the aqua background gradually
changes to a teal at the base.

92

VASE

Atlanta, Fulton County, 1906
Painted by C. W. Lycett
Made at Ceramic Art Company, Trenton, New Jersey
Belleek porcelain
11¾ inches high
Marks: Artist's palette and circle enclosing
entwined "CAC" above "BELLEEK" on bottom;
"C. W. Lycett" below roses
Descent in family of original owner
Lent by Mrs. Henry Latimer Collier, III

Edward Lycett of Staffordshire, England, established
the Faience Manufacturing Company in Green Point,
Brooklyn, in 1880. His son, William Lycett
(1855-1909), established a studio in Atlanta in 1883.
He taught china painting classes for amateurs, and
employed professional artists to decorate imported
porcelain blanks. William's cousin, C. W. Lycett, was
painting china at the Atlanta studio in 1906. Only
this vase and a pitcher have been found in Georgia
bearing C. W. Lycett's signature.[1]

This and two similar unmarked vases were originally owned by Antoinette Sheffield and Henry
Latimer Collier of Atlanta, who celebrated their
twenty-fifth wedding anniversary in 1906. Antoinette
Collier's descendants also own several pieces which
she painted with a gold rim and monogram.

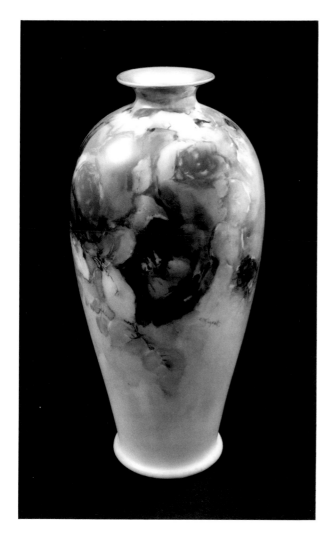

1. Carlyn Gaye Crannell, "In Pursuit of Culture: A History
   of Art Activity in Atlanta, 1847-1926," (Ph.D. disserta-
   tion, Emory University, 1981), p. 284.

93

PITCHER

Cox College, College Park, Fulton County, 1915
Painted by Marguerite Dyar Veach (1896-1981)
Made at Lenox China Company, Trenton, New Jersey
Belleek porcelain
15½ x 8¾ inches
Marks: Artist's palette and circle enclosing cursive
"L" above "BELLEEK" on bottom; "M. Dyar/Cox"
and "April 17, 1915" painted on bottom
Descent in family of maker
Lent by Mrs. Clyde J. Underwood

This tall pitcher with the grape motif and gold lizard
handle has the signature of the painter, the name of
her school, and the date of her work. The mark on the
base indicates that the ceramic body is belleek china
made in New Jersey.

Marquerite Dyar grew up in Bartow and Gordon
Counties. In 1913, she entered Cox College in Manchester (now College Park) where she studied art and
music. One of the art instructors there was Mary G.
Griggs (1871-1945), a student of William Lycett,
the Atlanta china painting teacher (see no. 92).[1]
Marguerite Veach's descendants own several pieces
which she painted while at Cox College: this pitcher,
a jardinière, and a lemonade service consisting of a
pitcher and six mugs. After graduating, Marguerite
Dyer married James Madison Veach in 1920 and lived
in Adairsville.

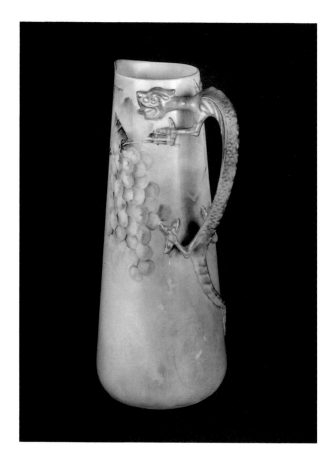

1. Carlyn Gaye Crannell, "In Pursuit of Culture: A History
of Art Activity in Atlanta, 1847-1926," (Ph. D. disserta-
tion, Emory University, 1981), p. 285.

94

TEA SERVICE

Athens, Clarke County, 1915
Painted by Kate McKinley Treanor Cobb (1886-1971)
Austrian and Bavarian porcelain
Teapot: 4 inches high
Marks: Wreath enclosing "C. & E.G./ROYAL/
AUSTRIA" on underside of sugar bowl, creamer, and
tea pot; "BAVARIA" on underside of cake plate and
oval tray; painter's marks "K.M.T.C./6/13/'15" on
base; owner's initial "B" on all pieces except tray
Descent in family of original owner
Lent by Ruth Barrow Bracewell

This five-piece tea service was decorated by Kate
Cobb while she was a student at the Lucy Cobb
Institute in Athens. She presented the set as a wedding
gift to her cousins, Clara and James Barrow; their
initial is painted in gold on each piece, except for the
serving tray (which also lacks the painter's initials
and date). Each piece is decorated with a wide gold
and white dogwood border.

THE HIGHLANDS REGION

The Highlands region covers the northern ten percent of the state. In the eastern Highlands, the Blue Ridge mountain chain forms high, steep, concentrated slopes covered by forests. The soil is rocky and poor; the rivers are fast, too narrow and shallow for most vessels. The western Highlands is an area of ridges and valleys with forests and fertile farm-lands. The soil here is ideal for crops, including cotton and apples. The Oostanaula and Etowah Rivers join in Rome to form the Coosa River, an important route through Alabama to the Gulf of Mexico.

Even before the first cession of Cherokee Indian lands in 1817, settlers from the back country of the Carolinas were homesteading in the eastern region of the Highlands, lands which were later officially dispersed through state lotteries. The first major towns, Gainesville (1818) and Clarkesville (1823), were founded. In 1829, gold was discovered near Dahlonega, and the promise of easy wealth attracted many more immigrants—from Tennessee, the Carolina mountains, and beyond. This area's economy rapidly expanded with the 1837 establishment of a United States Mint in Dahlonega, which became a major employer. Other than this, commerce in the eastern Highlands was limited until an extension of the Air-Line Railroad in 1856 linked Cornelia with Atlanta. The rail line stimulated commerce in Clarkesville, which was home to an iron foundry, apple and pear orchards, and inns catering to summer residents from the Tidewater region.

Settlers migrated to the western Highlands from South Carolina, up from the more established Piedmont communities of Georgia, and south from Kentucky and Tennessee. Rome was established in 1834 and by 1835 the entire western section of the Highlands had been ceded by the Indians. In the mid nineteenth century, coastal families built summer homes along the Etowah Valley from Rome to Cartersville and south towards Marietta. The economy of the western Highlands was agri-cultural. A railroad spur connecting Rome with the Western and Atlantic line in 1851 opened up trade routes north to Chattanooga and into the midwest, and Rome became the commercial center of the area.

Fieldwork for the Decorative Arts Survey was conducted in Toccoa and Clarkesville in the eastern Highlands and in Rome, Cartersville, Summerville, LaFayette, and Calhoun in the western part of the region. The entire Highlands region yielded only a small number of artifacts, undoubtedly because of the scattered and sparse settlement of the area and the generally weak economy. The small number of Highlands

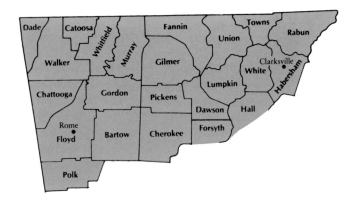

objects in the exhibition is proportional to the overall findings of the survey.

Furniture in the Highlands tended to be made primarily from local woods—walnut, yellow pine, chestnut, oak, and cherry, with poplar and yellow pine as secondary woods. Furniture from the eastern Highlands is frequently similar to Piedmont styles; in the west, furniture was often related to Kentucky and Tennessee examples. This demonstrates that settlement patterns influenced the appearance of furniture in the two Highlands sections. Some elaborate furniture was found, notably the work of Jarvis Van Buren from Clarkesville.[1] He used both imported mahogany and local timber to create fashionable furniture for the affluent summer residents. In the western Highlands, in Sonoraville, the survey found a family of cabinetmakers whose work spans six generations, from the 1840s to the present day (see nos. 100 and 105).

Highland textiles are generally more modest than work from other regions of the state. Although some imported chintz was used, crettone (an inexpensive glazed cotton) and calico were more frequently found in quilt tops. Alamance, a coarsely woven plaid cotton, was found in both quilt tops and backings. Wool was often used in crazy quilts.

The Highlands is home to one of the state's major pottery centers— Mossy Creek in White County. Potting families there included the Cravens, Davidsons, Dorseys, and Meaders. Because the story of this pottery has been thoroughly researched and published, it was not included in this exhibition.[2]

China painting was done in studios in Cartersville and possibly Rome in the late nineteenth century. The survey uncovered many examples still owned in the families of the women who painted them.

No locally made silver was found in the Highlands. The silver found here was from cities in other regions. However, the locally mined gold from veins below Dahlonega was coined at the United States Mint. A gold coin minted in Dahlonega is featured in the exhibition (no. 102). No artifacts have been found from the iron foundries which were operating in Clarkesville by 1828 and in Rome by the 1830s.

Early in the twentieth century, four important regional schools were established in the Highlands—The Berry School in Rome (founded in 1902), Nacoochee Institute (1903) and Rabun Gap Industrial School (1904), both in Rabun Gap, and the Tallulah Falls Industrial School in Tallulah Falls (1909). In addition to an academic curriculum, each taught vocational, domestic, and farming skills to the mountain students. A quilt stitched at The Berry School (no. 108) and a coverlet woven at Tallulah Falls Industrial School (no. 109) are in the exhibition.

1. Van Buren's work was not available for the exhibition.
2. John Burrison, *Brothers in Clay: The Story of Georgia Folk Pottery* (Athens, Ga.: University of Georgia Press, 1983), pp. 240 ff.

95

Blanket Chest

Pine Log, Bartow County, after 1836
Made by Martin Maxwell (1805-1882)
Yellow pine
24¼ x 38 x 18⅝ inches
Descent in family of maker
Lent by Ben R. Maxwell

This pine blanket chest was made by Martin
Maxwell, who moved from Elbert County to a farm
in Bartow County in 1836. His brother Thomas
Jackson Maxwell (1804-1869) was a cabinetmaker in
Elbert County.[1] Until recently, the present owners of
the chest also owned Maxwell's woodworking tools.

This is a common blanket chest form, with a lift
top and two drawers below. An unusual feature is that
the panels are beveled on the inside of the chest. The
stiles form modified bracket feet, a practice more
common in the Piedmont region than the Highlands.
The drawer joints are lapped and nailed rather than
dovetailed, which may indicate that the maker had
limited cabinetmaking skills. The owner believes that
the chest has never been painted.

1. William W. Griffin et al., *Neat Pieces: The Plain-Style
   Furniture of 19th Century Georgia* (Atlanta: Atlanta
   Historical Society, 1983), p. 10.

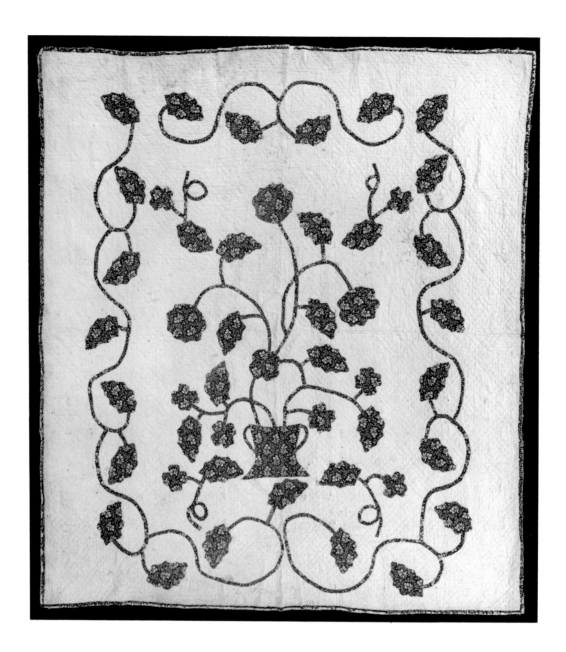

96

QUILT

Cumming, Forsyth County, 1837
Made by Nancy P. Holbrook Tribble (1825-1903)
Cotton
86¼ x 79 inches
Descent in family of maker
Lent by Robert B. and Winnie Tallant
Color illustration on page 62

Made by a twelve-year-old, this Vase of Flowers quilt has a charming, naive quality; the flowers and leaves are disproportionately large compared to the urn, and the border meanders casually, without the expected symmetry, crowding the central design. According to family history, Nancy Holbrook wove the background fabric from cotton which she picked and carded. The cards she used have descended in her family along with her quilt.

Vase of Flowers and Tree of Life designs were worked on eighteenth-century linsey-woolsey and crewelwork spreads. In the early decades of the nineteenth century, printed cottons were appliquéd to quilts in these patterns (see no. 5). This later example uses a blue and white floral calico, probably imported from England.

Nancy was one of nine children born to Juda and Absalom Holbrook, who lived on a 250-acre farm in Forsyth County. At the age of seventeen, she married James W. Tribble. Around 1854 Tribble left his wife and four children to seek his fortune in the California gold rush and never returned.

97

WORK TABLE

Possibly Stephens County, ca. 1850
Made by unknown artisan
Mahogany and mahogany veneers; yellow pine
25 x 21½ x 20 inches
Descent in family of original owner
Lent by Mr. and Mrs. Joe Prather

The maker of this table is unknown, but evidence links the table to Caleb T. Shaw, who moved to northeast Georgia from Massachusetts in the late 1840s. In the 1850 Census, Shaw was listed as a mechanic in Franklin County; in 1860 he was listed as a cabinetmaker. Shaw is known to have made furniture for Devereaux Jarrett of Traveler's Rest, near Toccoa in Stephens County, and he reportedly also made furniture for Jarrett's sons and daughter.[1] This table descended in the family of Jarrett's daughter, Sarah Ann, who was married to Joseph Jeremiah Prather of Toccoa.

Certain details of the table suggest a maker trained in New England. The legs extend through the frame to the table top, which is shaped to cover them, and the upper section of each leg is decorated with crisp ring turnings. This leg treatment was often used in New England on small tables and chests of drawers in the early nineteenth century; it has not been seen on other Georgia-made pieces. The bowfront design of the table and the use of mahogany and mahogany veneers, relatively common in New England, were unusual in the Georgia Highlands. Although imported mahogany was available through Savannah and Augusta, local walnut was the more common choice. The secondary wood used on this table is yellow pine, native to the South, which supports the conclusion that the table was made in Georgia by an artisan familiar with New England cabinetwork.

1. William W. Griffin et al., *Neat Pieces: The Plain-Style Furniture of 19th Century Georgia* (Atlanta: Atlanta Historical Society, 1983), pp. 9, 38.

98

CLOTHES PRESS

Chattooga County, ca. 1850
Made by unknown artisan
Yellow pine
75 x 48 x 19 inches
Descent in family of early owner
Lent by Mrs. John B. Echols, Sr.

This yellow pine clothes press was painted with Spanish brown paint, over which a black graining was crudely applied.[1] The upper portion has two interior shelves, and the lower portion, one. There is no evidence that the piece ever had a cornice.

This press is attributed to Chattooga County because of its long history in one family there. According to information provided by the family, the first owner probably was Hattie Mill Arnold of Subligna. The cupboard then passed to her brother and on to his daughter and her son, all from Chattooga County.

1. Early in the 1980s, an attempt was made to remove the original black graining, which had been mistaken for grease. The refinisher started with the door frames but stopped after encountering great difficulty.

99

CHEST OF DRAWERS

Cumming, Forsyth County, after 1850
Made by John Edmondson (1832-1921)
Walnut; yellow pine
41³⁄₈ x 38 x 17³⁄₈ inches
Descent in family of maker
Private collection

According to family history, this chest was made by
John Edmondson, a wagonmaker and blacksmith.
The 1850 Census records him as a 17-year-old farmer
living in Cumming with his widowed mother, Hannah.

Twenty years later he was listed as a wheelwright.

Edmondson's chest is stylistically similar to case
pieces from the Piedmont region, with string inlay on
the drawers and diamond-shaped inlaid escutcheons.
With the exception of the inlay, the construction is
simple. The drawers have nailed butt joints, with
squarehead machine-cut nails, and the legs are
formed as extensions of the side boards, sharply
chamfered on the side faces. There are only three tiers
of drawers—rather than the customary four—and each
tier is unusually deep.

100

Chest of Drawers

Sonoraville, Gordon County, 1849
Made by Jeremiah J. Dempsey (ca. 1810-1880s)
Cherry; tulip poplar and yellow pine
44½ x 43½ x 21½ inches
Marks: "D. S. Martin/Calhoun/Ga." in black
paint on back
Descent in family of original owner
Lent by Mrs. J. W. Butler

This chest is part of a set of bedroom furniture which also included a four-poster bed and a small table. Like this chest of drawers, both the bed and table have cherry as the primary wood (walnut would have been more commonly used in northwest Georgia). This set of furniture was commissioned by Mary Ann Amanda Graham and Claiborne Johnson Butler in 1849, when they settled in Sonoraville. The pieces remained together until Claiborne Butler's death in 1908, when they were divided among his descendants at an estate sale. Descendants of the Butlers cannot identify the D. S. Martin whose name is written on the back of the case.

The cabinetmaker, Jeremiah Dempsey, was the first of six generations of cabinetmakers residing in Sonoraville who made furniture for residents of Gordon County. Originally from South Carolina, Dempsey had moved to Floyd (now Gordon) County by 1840. The Manufacturing Census for 1880 lists him as a "cabinet workman" with two employees. A bookcase in the exhibition (no. 105), also from Sonoraville, was made by his son-in-law John Yule McEntyre, who was listed as a "sawyer" in the 1880 Census.

101

SIDEBOARD

Summerville, Chattooga County, ca. 1852-1861
Made by John Jacob Hosch (1810-1861)
Walnut; yellow pine and tulip poplar
56 x 69¼ x 24¾ inches
Marks: "This SideBoARD/BuiLt By JohN Hosch/
some Time BefoRe 1861" written in 1961 by Hosch
Holland, in pencil on back
Descent in family of maker
Lent by Pamela H. Bulman

This Empire-style sideboard is a standard American
form of 1815 to 1840. In the Georgia Highlands,
furniture of this style was usually large in scale with
bold columnar turnings and a heavy projecting upper
drawer. Approximately four dozen sideboards and
chests of drawers with similar features were recorded
for the survey in northwest Georgia (see no. 100).
This example was made of local woods.

According to family history, this sideboard was
made by John Jacob Hosch.[1] Along with a desk and

bookcase also by Hosch, it descended in the maker's
family in Chattooga County until 1983. The desk differs in style from the sideboard: it has straighter lines
and lighter proportions, inset paneled cupboard
doors, a slanted lift-top writing section, and square
tapered legs with mortise-and-tenon joints secured
with pegs.

John Jacob Hosch was born in Fairfield District,
South Carolina, in 1810; he moved to Chattooga
County from Walton County in 1852. Confederate
records confirm that he died in 1861 while serving
as a private in the Georgia Infantry.

1. The full pencil inscription on the back of the piece reads:
   "This Sideboard/built by John Hosch/some time before
   1861. He, John Hosch was later/killed in the Civil War/
   and brought home to/be buried in Trion/by Tom Foster
   who was/shot twice himself. This entered by/Hosch
   Holland 100/years later 1961. I am John Hosch's /great
   grandson/and at this writing I/am 60 years of age/and my
   mother/Minnie Foster Holland is 93."

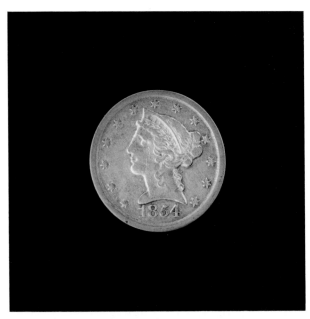

102

FIVE DOLLAR COIN

Dahlonega, Lumpkin County, 1854
Made at the United States Mint (1838-1861)
Gold
7/8 inch in diameter
Marks: "D" indicates Dahlonega mint
Lent by Sylvia G. Head

Ponce de Leon and later Hernando de Soto had found gold nuggets in the hills of Georgia in the sixteenth century. When substantial deposits were discovered in 1828 near Dahlonega, the strike triggered the first gold rush in the United States. On March 3, 1835, the Federal government passed a law establishing three branch mints outside Philadelphia—in New Orleans, Charlotte, and Dahlonega. The new mint in Dahlonega was permitted to coin only gold; the other two coined both gold and silver.[1] By April 1838, the first coins had been minted in an unfinished building using faulty equipment. But by then the local supply of gold was already declining.

The 1849 California gold rush was a mixed blessing to the Dahlonega mint. Many miners left Georgia to head west; some returned annually to sell their California gold to the mint. Within a few years, more California gold than native gold was being coined at Dahlonega. In 1854, 62,228 coins were minted, mostly half-eagles like this example.[2]

The mint was closed by the Confederate government in June 1861. The remaining bullion and coins were shipped to Charleston. The nitric acid used in processing the coins was used to make ammunition for the Confederate forces.

1. Sylvia Head and Elizabeth Etheridge, *The Neighborhood Mint: Dahlonega in the Age of Jackson* (Macon, Ga.: Mercer University Press, 1986), p. 15.
2. C. M. Birdsall, *The United States Branch Mint at Dahlonega, Georgia: Its History and Coinage* (Easley, S. C.: Southern Historical Press, 1984), p. 54.

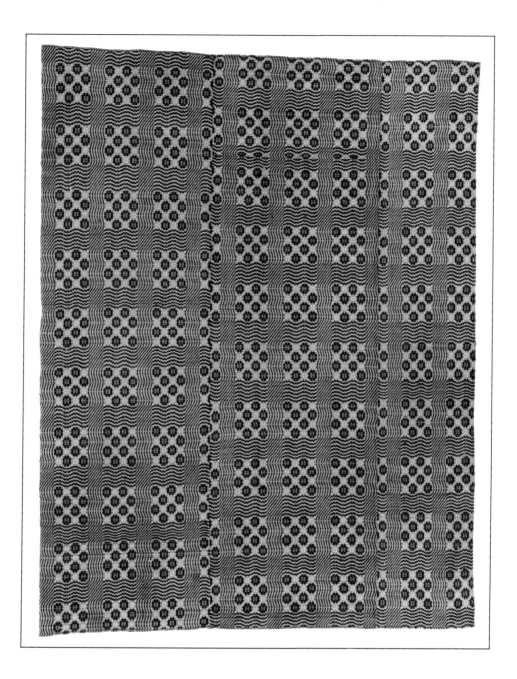

103

COVERLET

Pond Springs, Walker County, ca. 1880
Attributed to Julia Ann Clarkson Smith (1846-1916)
Wool and cotton
92 x 74 inches
Descent in family of maker
Lent by Mr. and Mrs. Charles Nelson Pursley

This slightly faded tri-color coverlet was woven in the Cat's Tracks and Snail Trails pattern. Green and peach wools contrast with beige cotton. The undulating lines—the twill separating the pattern—required extra skill in stringing the loom; the weft runs over and under several warps in an uneven sequence, produc-

ing this diagonal effect. Three separate woven lengths were stitched together to make the coverlet.

This coverlet and three others, woven in different patterns and colors, are attributed to Julia Ann Clarkson Smith, the daughter of Jane Hammond and James H. Clarkson. After her marriage to Nelson Duke Smith, Julia lived in McLemore's Cove and then on a farm in Pond Springs before settling in LaFayette, where her husband operated a feed store. The coverlets descended to the youngest of Mrs. Smith's five children, Eva Jane Smith, and are still owned by the family.

104

Cupboard

Chattooga County, ca. 1880
Made by James T. Avery (1855-1890)
Yellow pine
52½ x 42½ x 20¼ inches
Descent in family of maker
Lent by Mrs. John B. Echols, Sr.

According to family history, this cupboard was made by James T. Avery, a cotton grower. This example of his work demonstrates that Federal-style pieces, characterized by simple moldings and straight tapered legs, continued to be made in rural Georgia as late as 1880.

The cupboard has inset panels on its doors and sides and its interior is fitted with one shelf. Originally the piece stood about three inches taller, but the legs were cut off where the wood had rotted.

105

BOOKCASE

Sonoraville, Gordon County, ca. 1877
Made by John Yule McEntyre (1851-1932)
Walnut; yellow pine
91¼ x 46¼ x 22⅓ inches
Descent in family of original owner
Private collection
Color illustration on page 63

Masonic symbols are inlaid on the cornice and doors of this bookcase—a square and compass on the cornice and five-pointed stars at each of the corners of the upper case doors. The bookcase was made for Willie Ann Mansell (1856-1944) and Pleasant M. Watts (1856-1932) shortly after their marriage in 1877. Watts was a farmer and a member of the Calhoun Masonic lodge.

Family history records that the bookcase was made by John Yule McEntyre, a farmer in Sonoraville. McEntyre, listed by the 1880 Federal Census as a "sawyer," may have learned cabinetmaking from his father-in-law, Jeremiah J. Dempsey (see no. 100). A chest of drawers by McEntyre's son Phillip and a table by Phillip's son Kap were recorded in the Georgia Decorative Arts Survey. Kap's son and grandsons also became cabinetmakers—the fifth and sixth generations to practice the craft.

106

QUILT

Euharlee, Bartow County, ca. 1880
Made by Fannie L. Dodd Isbell (1852-1927)
Cotton
89 x 90 inches
Descent in family of maker
Lent by Fannie Laura Stowe

This Holly pattern appliquéd quilt is made of solid red and green fabrics introduced in the 1860s. Meticulous stitching simulates the veins of the leaves. Triple red sashing divides the quilt into a nine-block grid and forms the quilt's outer border.

The quilter, Fannie Dodd, was born in South Carolina. After her marriage in 1868 to George Munroe Isbell, she lived on a 200-acre farm in Euharlee.

107

QUILT

LaFayette, Walker County, ca. 1900
Made by Exa Montana Shahan Neal (1881-1976)
Cotton
79 x 67½ inches
Descent in family of maker
Private collection

This quilt is one of five documented by the survey as made by Exa Montana Shahan Neal. The bold tulips, leaves, and stems of this quilt are accented by rows of stitching just inside their edges. Although the flowers seem to float, they are organized in a grid. The maker used a crosshatch pattern for her background quilting. The patterns of Mrs. Neal's other quilts are

Feathered Star, Diamond and Square, Basket, and an embroidered crazy quilt. An overall grid format is common to all, but the fabrics vary. Two are quilted in the running shell pattern.

Family history records that Exa Montana Shahan Neal stopped quilting around 1908, when she married Reece Morton Neal, a merchant and farmer in West Armuchee in Walker County. After raising two children, Mrs. Neal taught school and later co-authored the history of the First Baptist Church in LaFayette. Her descendants also own six quilts made by her mother, Martha Jane Keown Shahan of Villanow, and one by her mother-in-law, Mary F. Morton Graham Neal of West Armuchee.

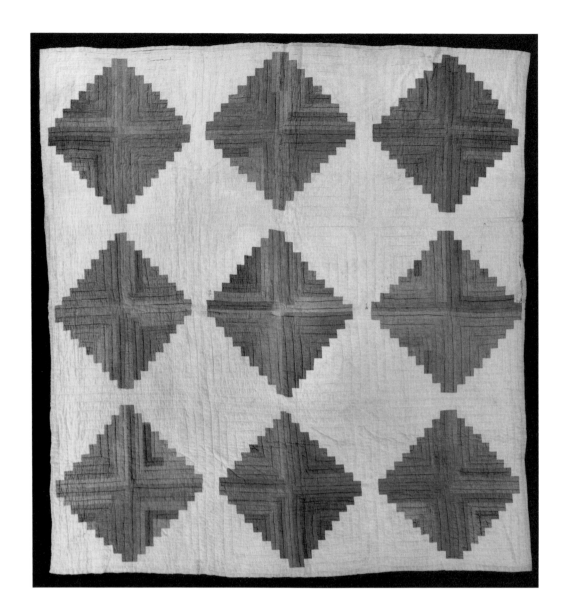

108

QUILT

Rome, Floyd County, ca. 1915
Made by students at The Berry School
Cotton
78¾ x 75 inches
The Martha Berry Museum of Berry College, Rome
Color illustration on page 64

Made by the students at The Berry School, this simple two-colored quilt is worked in a variation of the popular Log Cabin pattern. Strips of blue and white material were stitched together to form the diamonds. The fabrics used are believed to have been remnants of the materials used to make the students' uniforms: the blue used in the boys' work shirts, the white used in the cuffs and collars of the girls' blouses.

Martha McChesney Berry (1866-1942) established The Berry Schools (later Berry College) to provide an education for "mountain children of the Southern Appalachians." She established a day school on her family estate which in 1902 became a boarding school for boys. By 1909 a girls school had been added. In addition to offering an academic curriculum, Berry stressed the importance of domestic and farming skills. The program included handcraft courses such as weaving, sewing, chair-caning, basketry, and furniture-making.

In her 1925 speech accepting the Roosevelt Medal, Martha Berry said that her mission was "to free these young people and give them to America, strong of heart, mind and hand."[1]

1. Files, The Martha Berry Museum of Berry College, Rome, Georgia.

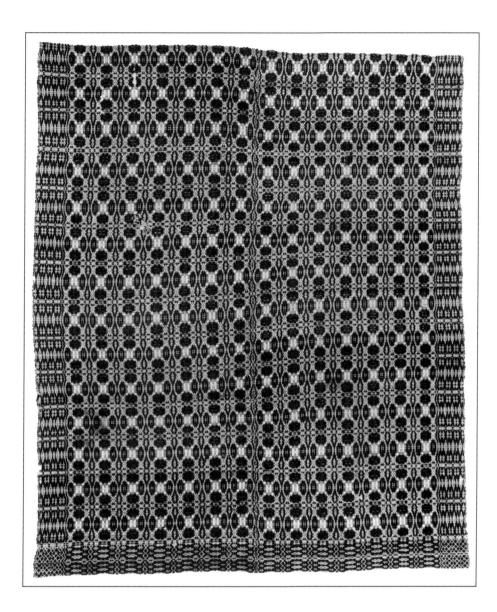

109

COVERLET

Tallulah Falls, Habersham County, ca. 1915
Made by students at Tallulah Falls Industrial School
Wool and cotton
78 x 66¾ inches
Tallulah Falls School
Color illustration on page 64

This coverlet, woven of pale fuscia and dark brown wools into a wheel motif, was made in two long narrow sections which were then stitched together. The twill border indicates a twentieth-century date.

Woven at the Tallulah Falls Industrial School, this coverlet is part of the tradition of handcrafts begun there in 1909 when the school was founded by the Georgia Federation of Women's Clubs. Like the Berry Schools and the Rabun Gap-Nacoochee School,[1] Tallulah Falls believed that students needed to learn practical skills, and therefore taught classes in weaving, basketry, shoe repair, and furniture-making in addition to traditional academic courses. The programs were comprehensive; a course in weaving would include raising the sheep, dyeing and spinning the wool, and threading and tying the loom. Finished products were marketed locally and in nearby towns in the region.

1. The Nacoochee Institute was founded in 1903 and the Rabun Gap Industrial School in 1905; they merged in 1927. See Carol Stevens Hancock, *Not by Magic But By Faith, Courage and Earnest Work* (Toccoa, Ga.: Commercial Printing Co., 1982), p. 21.

SELECTED BIBLIOGRAPHY

Primary Sources

United States Census Records for a number of counties were used, including the following years 1820, 1830, 1840, 1850, 1860, 1870, 1880, 1900, and 1910, to obtain data concerning original owners and artisans. The United States Census Georgia Manufacturing Schedules for 1820 and 1880 were used to verify and obtain information about the artisans working around the state. Wills, Inventories and Appraisements of Estates, and Bills of Sale were consulted for confirmation of family provenance.

Exhibition Catalogues

Ansa, Tina McElroy. *Not Soon Forgotten: Cotton Planters & Plantations of the Golden Isles of Georgia, 1784-1812.* St. Simons Island, Ga.: Coastal Georgia Historical Society, 1987.

Farnham, Katharine Gross, and Callie Huger Efird. *Georgia Collects American Silver, 1780-1870.* Atlanta: High Museum of Art, 1971.

Green, Henry D. *Furniture of the Georgia Piedmont before 1830.* Atlanta: High Museum of Art, 1976.

Griffin, William W., Florence P. Griffin, Sally W. Hawkins, and Deanne D. Levison. *Neat Pieces: The Plain-Style Furniture of 19th Century Georgia.* Atlanta: Atlanta Historical Society, 1983.

Harper, Suzanne, John Burrison, and Nancy Anderson. *Georgia Clay: Pottery of the Folk Tradition.* Macon, Ga.: Museum of Arts and Sciences, 1989.

Horton, Frank L., and Jan Garrett Hind. *The Museum of Early Southern Decorative Arts.* Winston-Salem, N.C.: Museum of Early Southern Decorative Arts, 1979.

Merritt, Carole. *Homecoming: African-American Family History in Georgia.* Atlanta: African-American Family History Association, Inc., 1982.

Mitchell, George. *In Celebration of a Legacy: The Traditional Arts of the Lower Chattahoochee Valley.* Columbus, Ga.: Columbus Museum of Arts and Sciences, 1981.

Moore, Ethel. *Decorative Arts of the Georgia Piedmont Before 1865.* Athens, Ga.: Georgia Museum of Art, 1976.

Reynolds, Elizabeth P. *Southern Comfort.* Atlanta: Atlanta Historical Society, 1978.

Smith, Jane Webb. *Georgia's Legacy: History Charted Through the Arts.* Athens, Ga.: University of Georgia Press, 1983.

Vlach, John Michael. *The Afro-American Tradition in Decorative Arts.* Cleveland: The Cleveland Museum of Art, 1978.

Wadsworth, Anna. *Missing Pieces: Georgia Folk Art, 1770-1976.* Atlanta: Atlanta Historical Society, 1976.

Books

Bell, Malcolm, Jr. *Major Butler's Legacy: Five Generations of a Slaveholding Family.* Athens, Ga.: University of Georgia Press, 1987.

Birdsall, C. M. *The United States Branch Mint at Dahlonega, Georgia: Its History and Coinage.* Easley, S.C.: Southern Historical Press, 1984.

Bolton, Ethel Stanwood, and Eva Johnston Coe. *American Samplers.* Princeton, N.J.: The Pyne Press, 1973.

Bouwman, Robert Eldridge. *Traveler's Rest and the Tugalo Crossroads.* Atlanta: Department of Natural Resources: Parks, Recreations and Historic Sites; Historic Preservation Section, 1980.

Brackman, Barbara. *Clues in the Calico: A Guide to Identifying and Dating Antique Quilts.* McLean, Va.: EPM Publications, Inc., 1989.

———. Encyclopedia of Pieced Quilt Patterns. 8 vols. Lawrence, Kans.: Prairie Flower Publishing, 1979-84.

Bragg, Lillian Chaplin. *Old Savannah Ironwork.* Savannah, Ga.: 1957.

Burrison, John A. *Brothers in Clay: The Story of Georgia Folk Pottery.* Athens, Ga.: University of Georgia Press, 1983.

Burroughs, Paul H. *Southern Antiques.* Richmond, Va.: Garrett & Massie, Inc., 1931.

Cashin, Edward J. *The Story of Augusta.* Augusta, Ga.: The Richmond County Board of Education, 1980.

Clarke, William Bordley. *Freemasonry in Georgia.* Macon, Ga.: Masonic Educational and Historical Commission of the Grand Lodge of Georgia, 1933.

Coleman, Kenneth, ed. *A History of Georgia.* Athens, Ga.: University of Georgia Press, 1977.

Cooper, Wendy A. *In Praise of America.* New York: Alfred A. Knopf, 1980.

Coulter, E. Merton. *Old Petersburg and the Broad River Valley of Georgia.* Athens, Ga.: University of Georgia Press, 1965.

Crannell, Carlyn Gaye. "In Pursuit of Culture: A History of Art Activity in Atlanta, 1847-1926." Ph.D. diss., Emory University, 1981.

Cutten, George Barton. *The Silversmiths of Georgia Together With Watchmakers & Jewelers—1730 to 1850.* Savannah, Ga.: Pigeonhole Press, 1958.

Davis, Harold E. *The Fledgling Province, Social and Cultural Life in Colonial Georgia, 1733-1776.* Chapel Hill, N.C.: University of North Carolina Press, 1976.

Eaton, Allen H. *Handicraft of the Southern Highlands.* New York: Dover Publications, Inc., 1973.

Fairbanks, Jonathan L., and Elizabeth Bidwell Bates. *American Furniture, 1620 to the Present.* New York: Richard Marek Publishers, 1981.

Galloway, David H. *Directory of the City of Savannah, for the Year 1849*. Savannah, Ga.: Edward C. Councell, 1848.

Gnann, Pearl Rahn. *Georgia Salzburgers and Allied Families*. Savannah, Ga.: Pearl Rahn Gnann, 1956.

Gross, Katharine Wood. "The Sources of Furniture Sold in Savannah, 1789-1815." Master's thesis, University of Delaware, 1967.

Hancock, Carol Stevens. *Not By Magic: But By Faith, Courage, and Earnest Work*. Toccoa, Ga.: Commercial Printing Company, 1982.

Head, Sylvia, and Elizabeth W. Etheridge. *The Neighborhood Mint: Dahlonega in the Age of Jackson*. Macon, Ga.: Mercer University Press, 1986.

Hood, Graham. *American Silver, A History of Style, 1650-1900*. New York: Praeger, 1973.

Jackson, Harvey H., and Phinizy B. Spalding, eds. *Forty Years of Diversity, Essays on Colonial Georgia*. Athens, Ga.: University of Georgia Press, 1984.

Jones, George Fenwick. *Henry Newman's Salzburger Notebooks*. Athens, Ga.: University of Georgia Press, 1966.

——. *The Salzburger Saga*. Athens, Ga.: University of Georgia Press, 1984.

Jones, George Fenwick, and Marie Hahn, eds. *Detailed Reports on the Salzburger Emigrants Who Settled in America . . . Edited by Samuel Urlsperger*. 9 vols. Athens, Ga.: University of Georgia Press, 1972-88.

Katzenberg, Dena S. *Baltimore Album Quilts*. Baltimore: Baltimore Museum of Art, 1981.

Koch, Mary Levin. "A History of the Arts in Augusta, Macon, and Columbus, Georgia, 1800-1860." Master's thesis, University of Georgia, 1983.

Kovel, Ralph M., and Terry H. Kovel. *A Directory of American Silver, Pewter and Silver Plate*. New York: Crown Publishers Inc., 1961.

Lane, Mills B., ed. *A Rambler in Georgia*. Savannah, Ga.: The Beehive Press, 1973.

Lewis, Bessie, and Mildred Huie. *Patriarchal Plantations of Saint Simons Island*. Darien, Ga.: 1974.

Linley, John. *The Georgia Catalog: Historic American Buildings Survey*. Athens, Ga.: University of Georgia Press, 1982.

McMorris, Penny. *Crazy Quilts*. New York: E. P. Dutton, 1984.

Martin, Van Jones, and William R. Mitchell, Jr. *Landmark Homes of Georgia, 1733-1983*. Savannah, Ga.: Golden Coast Publishing Company, 1982.

Mitchell, William R., Jr. *Landmarks: The Architecture of Thomasville and Thomas County, Georgia*. Thomasville, Ga.: Thomasville Landmarks, 1980.

Montgomery, Charles F. *American Furniture: The Federal Period, 1788-1825*. New York: The Viking Press, Inc., 1966.

Montgomery, Florence M. *Printed Textiles: English and American Cotton and Linens, 1700-1850*. New York: The Viking Press, Inc., 1970.

Moye, Sue McLendon. *Inventory of Early Stewart County Furniture*. Lower Chattahoochee Area Planning and Development Commission, 1978.

Myers, Robert Manson, ed. *The Children of Pride*. New Haven: Yale University Press, 1972.

100 Opinions of the American Press on Tallapoosa, Ga. and the Industrial Enterprise of the Georgia-Alabama Investment and Development Co. Boston: L. Barta & Co., Printers, 1891.

Phillips, Mary Walker. *Knitting Counterpanes, Traditional Coverlet Patterns for Contemporary Knitters*. Newtown, Conn.: Taunton Press, 1989.

Poesch, Jessie. *The Art of the Old South*. New York: Alfred A. Knopf, 1983.

Ramsey, Bets. *Old and New Quilt Patterns in the Southern Tradition*. Nashville, Tenn.: Rutledge Hill, 1987.

Ring, Betty. *American Needlework Treasures*. New York: E. P. Dutton, 1987.

Roberson, Ruth Haislip, ed. *North Carolina Quilts*. Chapel Hill, N.C.: University of North Carolina Press, 1988.

Rubin, Cynthia Elyce, ed. *Southern Folk Art*. Birmingham, Ala.: Oxmoor Press, 1985.

Solomon's Lodge Number 1, Free and Accepted Masons. *Handbook*. Savannah Ga.: Solomon's Lodge Number 1, Free and Accepted Masons, 1972.

Stillinger, Elizabeth. *The Antiques Guide to Decorative Arts in America, 1600-1875*. New York: E. P. Dutton & Co., Inc., 1972.

Swan, Susan Burrows. *Plain and Fancy: American Women and Their Needlework, 1700-1850*. New York: Holt, Rinehart and Winston, 1977.

Theus, Mrs. Charlton M. *Savannah Furniture, 1735-1825*. Savannah, Ga., 1967.

Newspapers

Augusta Chronicle and Gazette of the State
Augusta Herald
Brunswick Advertizer
Columbian Weekly Enquirer
Daily Georgian
Georgia Express, Athens
Georgia Gazette, Savannah
Georgia Journal, Milledgeville
Savannah Republican
Southern Banner, Athens

Articles

Coatney, G. Robert, and Robert G. Scholtens. "Georgia-Made Clocks." *Bulletin of the National Association of Watch and Clock Collectors, Inc.* 17 (October 1975): 454-77.

Comstock, Helen. "Furniture of Virginia, North Carolina, Georgia, and Kentucky." *Antiques* 61 (January 1952): 58-99.

Farnham, Katharine Gross, and Callie Huger Efird. "Early Silversmiths and the Silver Trade in Georgia." *Antiques* 99 (March 1971): 380-85.

Green, Henry D. "Furniture of the Georgia Piedmont Before 1830." *Art and Antiques* 5 (January-February 1982): 80-87.

———. "Georgia's Early Govenor's Mansion at Milledgeville, 1838-1868." *Antiques* 94 (December 1968): 864-67.

Swan, Mabel Munson. "Coastwise Cargoes of Venture Furniture." *Antiques* 55 (April 1949): 278-80.

Theus, Mrs. Charlton M. "Furniture in Savannah." *Antiques* 91 (March 1967): 364-67.

Warren, David, B. "Southern Silver." *Antiques* 99 (March 1977): 374-79.

Williams, James A. "Savannah Silver and Silversmiths." *Antiques* 91 (March 1967): 347-49.

INDEX OF GEORGIA ARTISANS

Aenchbacher, Gottlieb Nelson, no. 73
Avery, James T., no. 104
Barnett, Emaline Bridges, no. 54
Bentley, Green Berry, no. 69
Berry School, students, no. 108
Boatright, Melissa Veal, no. 42
Brumby Chair Company, no. 77
Carswell, John Franklin, attributed to, no. 62
Central State Penitentiary (Milledgeville), attributed
    to prisoners, no. 87
Ceramic Art Company, no. 92
Clark, Joseph Steadman, no. 60
Clay, Ann Legardere, no. 5
Clay, Eliza Caroline, no. 6
Cobb, Kate McKinley Treanor, painted by, no. 94
Danforth, IV, Thomas, attributed to, no. 45
David, Elizabeth, attributed to, no. 55
DeBrot, Mary Frances Victorine, no. 9
Dempsey, Jeremiah J., no. 100
Dennard, Frances Sarah Anne Crocker Solomon,
    no. 25
Dixie Glass Works, no. 89
Durrence, Elizabeth Smart Grice, no. 37
Eastman, F., no. 4
Edmondson, John, no. 99
Eve, Philoclea Edgeworth Casey, attributed to, no. 22
Fletcher, Dix, no. 68
Ferrell, Nancy Coleman, no. 61
Gentry, Azariah Denny, no. 58
Guill, Emmy Durham, no. 83
Hardman, Charlotta Barnett, no. 53
Harman, Absyllah Holmes Callaway, no. 80
Harp, James J., no. 31
Harris, Harold Charles "Chick," no. 84
Harris, James Wilson, no. 39
Hart, Anne Barnett, no. 65
Hempsted, Daniel Booth, no. 46
Hollingsworth, Joseph, no. 57
Hosch, John Jacob, no. 101
Inman, Margaret Josephine VanDyke, no. 78
Isbell, Fannie L. Dodd, no. 106
Johannsen, Caspar Hermann, no. 82
Jones, Everett Riley, no. 43
Kehoe and Company, no. 16
Ladeveze, Charles A., no. 72
Latimer, Mary Martia Sims, painted by, no. 91
LeBey, Jr., Christian David, attributed to, no. 12
LeBey, William Edward, no. 18
Lee, James Ellis, no. 63
Lycett, C. W., painted by, no. 92
Malaier, Mary Elizabeth Manley, no. 75
Marquand, Frederick, no. 8
Maxwell, Martin, no. 95
McEntyre, John Yule, no. 105
Mint, United States, no. 102
Muecke, Friedrich Wilhelm, no. 88

Müller, Freidrich Wilhelm, no. 1
Muse, Sarah Augusta Tucker, painted by, no. 34
Neal, Exa Montana Shahan, no. 107
Nichols, Sarah Davidson Cooper, no. 15
Ogier, John, no. 3
O'Kelley, William Alvin, no. 81
O'Neal, Basil, no. 44
Orme, Kate Harman, no. 79
Pattison and Sons Foundry and Machine Shop,
    attributed to, no. 33
Pearson, Narcissa Caroline Woodall, no. 85
Peters, Sarah A. Davis, no. 35
Phillips, Georgina Cohen, no. 14
Render, Mary Jane Dixon, no. 67
Riviere, R. Elizabeth Belah, no. 64
Sage and Company, A., assembled by, no. 11
Second Baptist Church (Savannah), no. 13
Sikes, Charlotte Burch, no. 30
Slappey, Alexander G., no. 21
Smith, Julia Ann Clarkson, no. 102
Smith, William Sheppard, no. 74
Stephens, Jane Albritton Jones, no. 32
Stevens Brothers & Company, no. 76
Tallulah Falls Industrial School, students, no. 109
Timmerman Jug Company, no. 38
Tribble, Nancy P. Holbrook, no. 96
Tucker, Sarah Elizabeth Hardison, no. 40
Variety Works, Reynolds, Hargrave and Sons or
    Edward Orlando Thompson, no. 36
Variety Works (Madison), no. 86
Veach, Marguerite Dyar, painted by, no. 93
Wells, Mary Elizabeth Vallotton, no. 7
Wilkins, John D., no. 10
Willingham, Anne Lewis Rushkin, no. 90
Wing, Lewis H., probably engraved by, no. 71
Wise, Laura Rachel Addy, no. 41